Cambridge Primary

Hodder Cambridge Primary
Science

Learner's Book

Stage 2

Deborah Herridge
Series editor: Rosemary Feasey

HODDER
EDUCATION
AN HACHETTE UK COMPANY

Acknowledgements

The Publisher is extremely grateful to the following schools for their comments and feedback during the development of this series:

Avalon Heights World Private School, Ajman

The Oxford School, Dubai

Al Amana Private School, Sharjah

British International School, Ajman

Wesgreen International School, Sharjah

As Seeb International School, Al Khoud

The publisher would like to thank the following for permission to reproduce copyright material.

p.6 Glaw et al. 2012, PLoS One; **p.22** Susan Evans http://susanevans.org/blog/hands-on-activities-for-weather/castlesusan@gmail.com; **p.70** From 101 Great Science Experiments (London: DK, 2015). Copyright © Dorling Kindersley Ltd., 1993. Reproduced by permission of Penguin Random House UK; **p.115** http://www.tynesidebb.org/picture.asp?location=1morpeth&eventid=821&pictureid=1137.

Photo acknowledgements

p.6 © DPA Picture Alliance Archive/Alamy Stock Photo; **p.7 tl** © Sam74100/123rf; **p.7 tr** © Audrey Snider-Bell/123rf; **p.7cl** © Vladimir Kramin/123rf; **p.7 c** © Maksim Kostenko/123rf; **p.7 c** © Jiri Vaclavek/123rf; **p.7 c** © Khatawut Chaemchamras/123rf; **p.7 c** © Dontree Malaimarn/123rf; **p.7 cr** © Marigranula/123rf; **p.7 bl** © Martesia Bezuidenhout/123rf; **p.7 br** © Marco Mayer/123rf; **p.8** © Andamanse/123rf; **p.9** © Ingram Publishing Limited/Animals Gold Vol 1 CD 3; **p.12** © Oote Boe 1/Alamy Stock Photo; **p.13** © Aberration/123rf; **p.14 t** © Michael Warwick/123rf; **p.14 b** © Lindsay Franklin/Shutterstock; **p.16 t** © Leungchopan/Fotolia; **p.16 b** © Blue Orange Studio/123rf; **p.17 c** © Joel Sartore/Getty Images; **p.17 b** © Christopher Ison/123rf; **p.20** © John Cancalosi/Getty Images; **p.21** © Tatyana Tomsickova/123rf; **p.22 t** © Nelli Syrotynska/123rf; **p.22 c, b, p.143** © Hachette UK; **p.23** © Ian Hinchliffe/Alamy Stock Photo; **p.24 t** © Steffen Niclas/Fotolia; **p.24 b** © Pat138241/123rf; **p.25** © Michael Steden/Getty Images/iStockphoto/Thinkstock; **p.26** © Phil Wills/Alamy Stock Photo; **p.28 t p.141** © A. Karnholz/Fotolia; **p.28 c** © Emmanuel Lacoste/Alamy Stock Photo; **p.30 tl** © Jantima Plablabpo/123rf; **p.30 tc** © Belchonock/123rf; **p.30 tc** © YurakP/123rf; **p.30 tr** © Mechanik/123rf; **p.30 cl** © Sermsak Sukwajikhlong/123rf; **p.30 cr** © 罗 宏志/123rf; **p.30 bl** © Nikkos/Shutterstock; **p.30 br** © Sergei Bogomyakov/123rf; **p.32** © Panther Media GmbH/Alamy Stock Photo; **p.33** © Maurisole/Fotolia; **p.36 tl ,br** © Tyler Boye/Shutterstock; **p.36 tr** © Getty Images/iStockphoto/Thinkstock; **p.36 bl** © Alexlukin/123rf; **p.37, p140** © Igor Kali/Fotolia; **p.39** © Krzysztof Slusarczyk/123rf; **p.42 t** © Ingram Publishing Limited/Scenery Backdrops Gold Vol 1 CD 2; **p.42 c** © Emmeci74/123rf; **p.42 cr** © Cokemomo/123rf; p.42 b © Anikasalsera/123rf; **p.43 tl** © Fabrizio Troiani/123rf; **p.43 tr** © Sakdinon Kadchiangsaen/123rf; **p.43 b** © Angellodeco/123rf; **p.43 r** © Antonio Violi/Alamy Stock Photo; **p.44** © Brooke Becker/Fotolia; **p.46 t** © Mikhail Avdeev/123rf; **p.46 b** © Stephen Denness/123rf; **p.48 t** © Mats Tooming/Fotolia; **p.48 bl** © Koosen/123rf; **p.48 bc** © Ilya Akinshin/123rf; **p.48 bc** © Andrius Gruzdaitis/123rf; **p.49** © Costasz/123rf; **p.51** © Belchonock/123rf; **p.53 l** © STA/Shutterstock; **p.53 r** © Mohammed Anwarul Kabir Choudhury/123rf; **p.54 t** © HadelProductions/Getty Images; **p.57** © FFF39/123rf; **p.58 tl** © Warayoo/123rf; **p.58 tr** © V.J Matthew/123rf; **p.58 cl** © Photobalance/123rf; **p.58 cr** © Somchai Somsanitangkul/123rf; **p.58 bl** © Bcrbnbvtw/123rf; **p.58 bc** © Server/123rf; **p.58 br** © Boris Terekhov/123rf; **p.59** © Mark/KA/iStock/Thinkstock/Getty Images; **p.64** © Artem Merzlenko/Fotolia; **p.66** © Oleksandr Farion/123rf; **p.67** © Artem Merzlenko/Fotolia; **p.68** © Pictures News/Fotolia; **p.73** © Jessica of Balancing Everything/Getty Images; **p.78 t** © SeanPavonePhoto/Fotolia; **p.78 b** © Anton Balazh/Shutterstock; **p.80** © Jun.SU/Fotolia; **p.81 t** © Allan Swart/123rf; **p.81 b** © Vvoennyy/123rf; **p.82 t** © Steven Heap/123rf; **p.82 b** © Chatnakorn Chuankul/123rf; **p.83 t, p.120** © StockTrek/Photodisc/Getty Images/Science, Technology & Medicine 2 54; **p.83 b** © Justin Kase Zsixz/Alamy Stock Photo; **p.86 cr** © Maximilian Weinzierl/Alamy Stock Photo; **p.86 cl** © Bluegreen Pictures/Alamy Stock Photo; **p.87 t** © Ben Nottidge/Alamy Stock Photo; **p.87 b** © Evgeniy Meyke/123rf; **p.89** © Trevor Slauenwhite/Fotolia; **p.91** © Cristi180884/Fotolia; **p.92** © Andrey Chernikov/123rf; **p.93** © Copacabana/Shutterstock; **p.94** © Loganban/123rf; **p.96** © Eladora/123rf; **p.98** © Dejan Krsmanovic/Alamy Stock Photo; **p.100** © Nikolai Sorokin/Fotolia; **p.102** © Warren Goldswain/123rf; **p.107** © Tejmos/Shutterstock; **p.109** © Monkey Business Images/Shutterstock; **p.112** © Canit Kaewtubnil/123rf; **p.116** © Elizaveta Galitckaia/123rf; **p.117 (both)** © Ivydale Science & Technology Service; **p.118 t** © NASA Magann/Fotolia; **p.118 b** © Photodisc/Getty Images/Business & Industry 1; **p.119 tl** © Baldas1950/Fotolia; **p.119 tr** © Romolo Tavani/Fotolia; **p.124** © Jovannig/123rf; **p.126** © Hanohiki/123rf; **p.131 l**, p.142 © David Cole/Alamy Stock Photo; **p.131 r** © StockTrek/Photodisc/Getty Images/ Science, Technology & Medicine 2 54; **p.133** © Digital Vision/Getty Images/Astronomy & Space DV25; **p.134** © Getty Images/iStockphoto/Thinkstock; **p.136** © NASA.

t = top, *b* = bottom, *l* = left, *r* = right, *c* = centre

Practice test exam-style questions and sample answers have been written by the author(s).

Note: While every effort has been made to check the instructions for practical work described in this book carefully, schools should conduct their own risk assessments in accordance with local health and safety requirements.

Every effort has been made to trace all copyright holders, but if any have been inadvertently overlooked the Publishers will be pleased to make the necessary arrangements at the first opportunity.

Although every effort has been made to ensure that website addresses are correct at time of going to press, Hodder Education cannot be held responsible for the content of any website mentioned in this book. It is sometimes possible to find a relocated web page by typing in the address of the home page for a website in the URL window of your browser.

Hachette UK's policy is to use papers that are natural, renewable and recyclable products and made from wood grown in sustainable forests. The logging and manufacturing processes are expected to conform to the environmental regulations of the country of origin.

Orders: please contact Bookpoint Ltd, 130 Milton Park, Abingdon, Oxon OX14 4SB.

Telephone: (44) 01235 827720. Fax: (44) 01235 400454. Lines are open from 9.00–500,

Monday to Saturday, with a 24 hour message answering service. You can also order through our website www.hoddereducation.com

© Deborah Herridge 2017

Published by Hodder Education

An Hachette UK Company

Carmelite House, 50 Victoria Embankment, London EC4Y 0DZ

Impression number   5 4 3 2 1

Year   2019 2018 2017

Cover illustration © Steve Evans

Illustrations by Samantha van Riet, Gabriel Metcalf, Jeanne du Plessis and Vian Oelofsen

Typeset in FS Albert 17 on 19pt by IO Publishing CC

Printed in Slovenia

A catalogue record for this title is available from the British Library

9781471883835

Contents

Being a scientist

What does a scientist do?

Scientists are interested in things around them. They have ideas and ask questions. They test their ideas to find answers.

Scientists observe things closely. They use their senses. They record what they find.

Scientists try to keep things fair when they test an idea.

Scientists observe many things. They ask: How are they the same? How are they different? They group things such as animals in the sea.

Scientists find information in books and on the internet. They read a lot. They share what they learn.

Scientists observe things to compare them.

Scientists measure things. They look for patterns in their results.

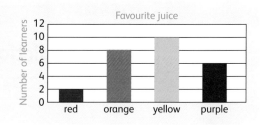

Favourite juice

Number of learners: 12, 10, 8, 6, 4, 2, 0 — red, orange, yellow, purple

How to do a fair test

A fair test is a way to investigate a scientific question.
To carry out a fair test, scientists must think about certain things.

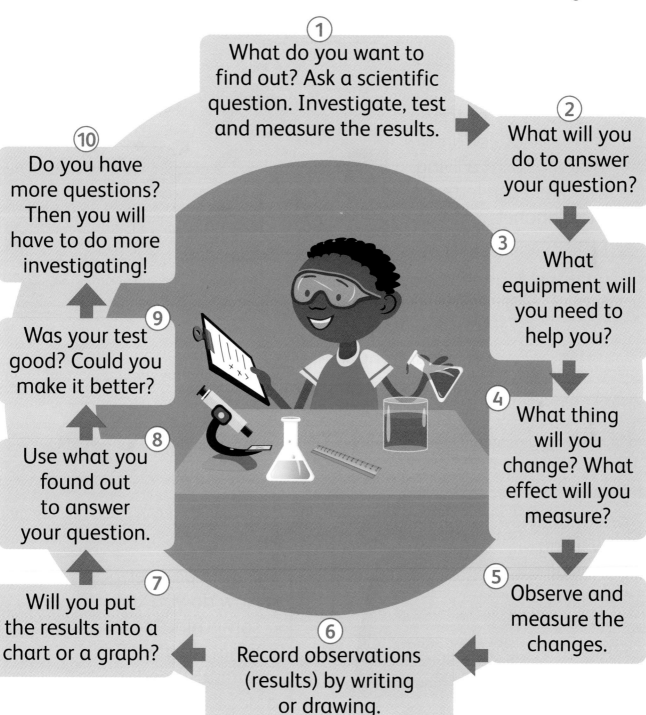

① What do you want to find out? Ask a scientific question. Investigate, test and measure the results.

② What will you do to answer your question?

③ What equipment will you need to help you?

④ What thing will you change? What effect will you measure?

⑤ Observe and measure the changes.

⑥ Record observations (results) by writing or drawing.

⑦ Will you put the results into a chart or a graph?

⑧ Use what you found out to answer your question.

⑨ Was your test good? Could you make it better?

⑩ Do you have more questions? Then you will have to do more investigating!

I am alive!

1

What do you know about living things?

a Make a list of all the living things you know. Then try to list a living thing for each letter of the alphabet.

b How many living things are there around your school? Make a list.

Remember, plants are also living things!

Did you know?

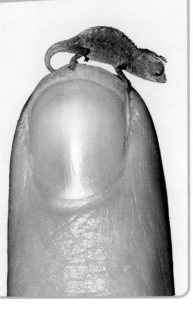

Scientists are finding new living things all the time. This tiny chameleon was discovered in 2012.

Talk partners

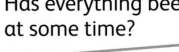

Talk to a partner.
a How do you know if something is alive or not?
b What do plants and animals need to live?
c Has everything been alive at some time?

Alive or not?

Think like a scientist!

Scientists often try to **sort** things into **groups**. We can **classify** things by what they look like or by what they do.

Scientific words
sort
groups
classify
similar
different

1

Look at the pictures. Work in a small group to sort these things.

baby

scorpion

car

wooden chair

banana plant

cloud

soft toy

cactus

metal knife and fork

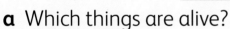
cooked rice

a Which things are alive?

b Which things are not alive?

c How did you decide?

d Can you think of another group?

2

Look at the groups you made in Activity 1.

a What is **similar** (almost the same) about the things in your group?

b What is **different**?

Talk partners

a Talk to a partner about things that were once living, but are not living now.

b Make a list.

Challenge yourself!

Did you know that some clothes were once plants? Some of our clothes were once alive! Find out about cotton, flax and bamboo.

Sorting and grouping living things

Scientific word
invertebrates

Think like a scientist!

Living things can be very different.
A snake is a living thing.
So is a grasshopper, a plant and a tiger.
Humans are also living things.

We call tiny creatures such as insects, spiders, worms and snails **invertebrates**.
They are all animals.

Talk partners

It can be difficult to tell living things apart.
Look at this picture.
Is it a plant or an animal?

1

Sort these living things into groups.
Ask a partner to guess how you sorted them.

a Explain to your partner how you sorted them into groups.

b Have you and your partner sorted them in the same way?

c How many ways can you sort the living things? Make a list.

What is the environment?

Think like a scientist!

Scientific word
environment

Animals and plants are living things.
Different plants and animals live in different places in the world.

The **environment** is everywhere where animals and plants live.
Animals and plants grow in the environment.
They make new plants and animals.

Not all environments are the same.
Some plants and animals can only
live in certain environments.
These penguins live in the Antarctic.

penguins in the Antarctic

1

a What lives in these environments? Find out and make a list.

tropical rainforest

polar regions

desert

coral reef

b Kai and Ali have started a list. Copy the table. Add another environment.
Add more animals and plants to this list. Circle the plants.

Tropical rainforest	Polar regions	Desert	Coral reef	
jaguar	reindeer	salt bush	seagrass	
orchid			parrotfish	

Your environment: who lives here?

Think like a scientist!

You know that different animals and plants live in different environments.

Even in your environment, different animals and plants live in different places.

1

Think about where you live. That is your environment.

a Describe the land. Is it flat or are there mountains? Is it grassy or sandy?

b Is it hot or cool? Does it rain a lot or is it very dry?

c Write about your environment. Then draw a picture of what you wrote.

Be careful ⚠️

Wash your hands if you have touched animals, plants or **soil**.

Scientific words

soil   prediction   compare

2

You are going on safari (a hunt) around your school environment!

a Make a **prediction**. Which plants and animals do you think you will find? Write a list.

b Walk around your school environment with a partner.

c Draw and label all the living things that share your environment.

d Count how many different animals you find.

e How many different plants do you notice?

f **Compare** your list to your prediction. Did you find everything you expected to find?

Which place is best?

1

a Make a chart of the animals (invertebrates) you found on your safari in Activity 2 on page 10. Look at the bar chart that Noor and Sara made. Do something similar.

> **Think like a scientist!**
>
> There are areas in the local environment that some animals and plants prefer.

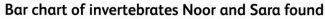

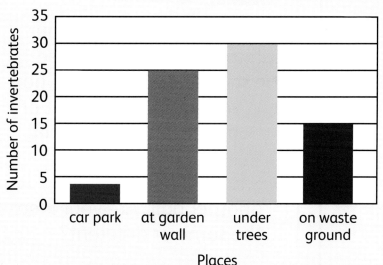

Bar chart of invertebrates Noor and Sara found

(y-axis: Number of invertebrates, 0 to 35; x-axis: Places — car park, at garden wall, under trees, on waste ground)

> Where did Noor and Sara find the most animals? Can you think of a reason why?

b Where did you find the most animals?

c Compare the animals you found with those of another group. Are the animals the same or are they different?

d Why are some different? Were those animals in different places?

> **Did you know?**
>
> Scientists estimate that there are ten quintillion insects in the world. That is a '10' with 18 zeros! How many insects did you find around school?

Habitats and homes

Think like a scientist!

Who lives where?

Would a polar bear survive … in the desert?

Have you ever seen a whale … living in a tree?

1

Did you find any micro-habitats on your safari in Activity 2 on page 10?

Scientific words

habitat

stone

micro-habitat

Talk partners

Talk to a partner about your habitat or home. Try to use the scientific words in the box.

a What does your habitat or home have that you need to live?

b Share your ideas with another pair. Are your ideas the same or different?

All living things live in their own special place that suits them best.

We call the home of a plant or animal its **habitat**.

Some habitats are big, such as rainforests or seas. Other habitats are tiny, such as under a **stone**. These tiny habitats are called **micro-habitats**. All habitats have things that animals or plants need to live.

micro-habitat of ants

Everything you need

Think like a scientist!

Your home is a habitat. You are an animal. You have needs like other animals. Your habitat is a place that gives you everything you need to live.

1

a Savi has started a chart about her home. Start a chart for your home.

b What would happen if we had none of these things? Would we survive?

c Think of an animal you found on your safari. Fill in a chart for that animal. Does it need the same things as you?

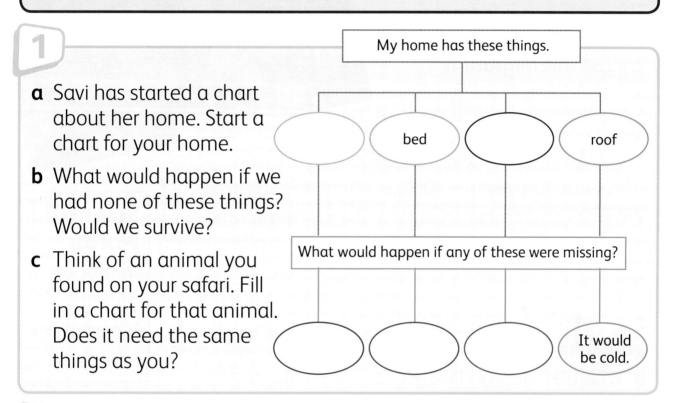

My home has these things.

bed   roof

What would happen if any of these were missing?

It would be cold.

2

a Draw and label a picture of your perfect home.

b What special things would you have in it? What things in your home do you *need* to live? Which things are just nice to have?

Some animals carry their homes around with them. Look at the hermit crab.

hermit crab

Moving home or staying in

Think like a scientist!

Some animals move to a new habitat when the weather gets colder.
They move to find food or shelter in the colder months.
We call this **migration**.

Every year, millions of monarch butterflies **migrate**.
They travel a long way. In winter they fly from cold Canada to warm Mexico where it is summer.
When it is summer in Canada, they migrate back.

monarch butterflies

Scientific words

migration
migrate
hibernation
hibernate

1

a Find Canada and Mexico on a map or globe.

b Where in the world would you like to migrate? How far away from your home is the place?

You will need...
• world map or globe

Talk partners

Some animals sleep through the colder months of the year. This is called **hibernation**. Some bears, lemurs and bats **hibernate** in winter when food is hard to find. Talk to a partner. Do humans need to migrate or hibernate when the weather changes?

brown bear

Animals in danger

Think like a scientist!

Sometimes an environment changes. This can put animals and plants in danger. They can become **extinct** if their environment changes too much. Extinct means that there are no more of that **species** (type) of animal or plant.

Dodos were birds that lived on the island of Mauritius in the Indian Ocean. Mauritius was their only home.

Dodos could not fly. When explorers arrived, they caught the dodos and ate them.

More people came to live on the island. They brought cats, rats and monkeys. These animals also ate the dodos and their eggs. Soon there were very few dodos.

Now there are no dodos at all. People and animals changed the environment. Dodos became extinct.

Find out about other extinct species.

Scientific words
extinct
species

Challenge yourself!

What changes in the environment made dodos extinct? Imagine that you could go back in time. What would you do to protect the dodo?

Endangered animals

Scientific word
endangered

Think like a scientist!

Some living animals are in danger of becoming extinct. We call these animals **endangered**.

Talk partners

Ace and Zara are talking about a rainforest.

a Talk to a partner. Who do you think is right?

b Share your ideas with another pair. Do you all agree?

1

Look at these animals. They are endangered. Find out why they might become extinct.

a
giant panda

b
hawksbill turtle

People are destroying the forest and the animals' homes.

Cutting down the trees gives the rainforest workers the jobs and money they need.

Rainforest plants are used in medicine. If we destroy them, we might not have new medicines.

There are lots of plants left in the rainforest.

2

a Find or draw a picture of an endangered animal.

b Add a speech bubble to your animal. Write what you imagine it would ask you to do to save it from extinction.

Changes in the environment

Think like a scientist!

Humans can change or damage an environment. 'HIPPO' can help you to understand how.

(H) for **Habitats being destroyed**. Humans chop down forests to make room for farming. The forest animals lose their habitats.

(I) for **Invasion!** Sometimes humans move plants or animals to environments where they do not belong. They may take over the environment from the plants and animals that normally live there.

(P) for **People**. More and more humans are being born. People compete with animals for space and food.

This pelican is covered in oil.

(P) for **Pollution**. Oil spills can damage the environment.

(O) for **Overhunting**. Some people hunt animals for their skins, horns or tusks. Many species become endangered.

Challenge yourself!

Cane toads were moved to Australia.
Find out what happened.

Scientific word
pollution

1

The South African black rhino is hunted for its horn.
Find out more.

2

The Worldwide Fund for Nature works to protect endangered animals. Find out more.

Cleaning up!

Think like a scientist!

Humans can damage the environment but they can also help to protect it.

Be careful ⚠

Oil can be slippery.
Clean up any spills.

1

You will need...

- clear plastic cup
- water
- cooking oil (the darker in colour it is, the better)
- small clean feathers
- soap

Work in a small group. Re-create an oil slick. Find out what happens to birds that get caught in oil.

a Pour some water into a clear cup.

b Carefully pour some cooking oil on the water. What do you notice?

c Describe your feather. What does it feel like?

d Predict what will happen to the feather if it is covered in oil. What will it look and feel like?

e Dip the feather through the oil and water. What does it look and feel like now?

f Compare it to a dry, clean feather. How is it different?

g Think about how to remove the oil from the feather. Try your idea.

Protecting your environment

Think like a scientist!

Plants and animals in your environment may be in danger. We must protect the environment to stop living things from becoming extinct.

1

Go back to page 10. Do you remember looking for animals around school?

a Are any of them at risk (in danger)? Why? What could be a risk to their survival?

b What about animals in your country? Are any in danger? Why?

c How could you help to protect the plants and animals in your school and country?

d Work with a partner. Make a poster to explain one thing we could all do to help to protect our environment.

Talk partners

Talk to a partner.
What could you do to make your school environment a better place for wildlife?

a Make a list of your ideas.

b Share your ideas with others.

c Choose the best idea and make it happen!

d Write about what you did and why.

19

What can I do?

Think like a scientist!

Scientific word
recycle

We can all do something to help to care for and protect our environment.

We can start with small changes. Over time, small changes add up to become a big change!

Talk partners

Talk to a partner. What could you do to help to protect the environment? Could you:

a walk to school or ride a bike rather than going by car?

b share a car with others to use less fuel?

c plant a tree or create a safe habitat for invertebrates?

d **recycle** your plastic bags by using them more than once?

e take your rubbish home? Rubbish we throw away carelessly can hurt animals.

f what else could you do to help the environment?

This white stork needs help to free it from the plastic bag.

1

a Write a script for a radio show. The script should encourage people to make small changes to care for and protect the environment.

b Perform it for your class.

What's the weather like today?

Scientific words
heat
Sun

Think like a scientist!

The weather is part of the environment. It is made up of three things:

- **heat** from the **Sun** (sunshine)
- moving air (wind)
- water (rain, hail, mist or snow).

All of these together give us the weather.

In some countries, the weather does not change much each day. In other places it changes a lot.

1

What is the weather like today where you live? Draw a picture.

2

a What is your favourite type of weather? Why?

b Write some sentences about the kind of weather you like.

3

a Work in a small group. Draw symbols (simple pictures) for the weather in your country.

b Make a weather recording chart showing sunshine, rain and wind.

c What other type of weather can you record? Design a symbol.

d Record the weather for each day on your chart.

Measuring rainfall

Think like a scientist!

Scientific words
rain gauge
record

Rain is water falling from clouds.
In some parts of the world it rains a lot. In other places it hardly rains. Sometimes water falls as sleet, snow or hail.

Scientists measure how much rain falls every day. They use a **rain gauge**. Make a rain gauge like this one. Then measure how much rain falls.

You will need...
- two-litre plastic bottle
- sticky tape
- ruler
- scissors
- paper
- pen

- Ask an adult to help you to cut the top off an empty two-litre plastic bottle.

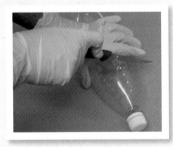

- Put the top part of the bottle upside down into the bottom to make a funnel.

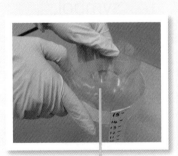

funnel

- Make marks on the side of the bottle to measure how much rain falls. Should the marks be close together or far apart? How will you decide?

- Place your rain gauge outside. Find a safe place in the open where your rain gauge will not be knocked over.

- **Record** your measurements at regular intervals (after regular amounts of time).

Rainfall charts

Think like a scientist!

Too much rain can lead to floods. Floods can damage bridges and roads if rivers overflow.

Too little rain can cause droughts. Plants die without enough water.

1

Bilal measured the rain every day. Each day, he collected rain in a different plastic cup.

| day 1 | day 2 | day 3 | day 4 | day 5 |

He made a chart of his results.

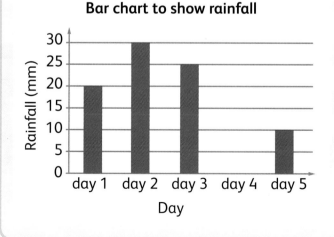

Bar chart to show rainfall

a Which day had no rain?

b When was there the most rain?

c How much rain was there in total?

2

a Look outside. Are there any clouds in the sky? What do they look like?

b How much of the sky is covered with clouds? All? None? Half?

c How can you record this on your weather chart?

Measuring the wind

Scientific word
scale

Think like a scientist!

Wind is the movement of air. This windsock shows the direction of the wind.

Wind blows from the directions on a compass – North, South, East and West.

Talk partners

Talk to a partner.
a Is the wind always the same?
b What changes about the wind on different days?
c What would we need to measure?

1

You will need...
• compass   • chalk
• play bubbles

a Find the compass directions outside with your teacher.

b Chalk the points of the compass on the ground.

c Blow some play bubbles outside.

d What can the bubbles show you about the direction of the wind?

e Decide how you will record the strength of the wind.

f What can the bubbles show you about how strong the wind blows?

g Make up a **scale** to describe how strong the wind is. It could go from 'cannot feel any wind' to 'so strong it is difficult to stand'.

Sunshine

Think like a scientist!

Scientists who study the weather are called **meteorologists**.
They use special sunshine recorders to measure how much sunlight there is each day.

sunshine recorder

1

a Do you feel warm when you stand in a sunny spot?

b Stand outside in a sunny place. Then stand in a shady place. How do you feel? Hotter or cooler?

2

We measure **temperature** by using a **thermometer**.

Thermometers have scales on them. The higher the number, the hotter the temperature.

- 40 °C very hot
- 30 °C hot
- 20 °C warm
- 10 °C cool
- 5 °C cold
- 0 °C freezing

Look at these thermometers.

a Which one is in the hottest place?

b Which one is in the coolest place?

A: 50 45 40 35 30 25 20 15 10 5 0

B: 50 45 40 35 30 25 20 15 10 5 0

Scientific words
meteorologists   temperature
thermometer

3

You will need...
- thermometer

Measure the temperature in your playground at different times of the day. Is it always the same?

Weather forecasting

Think like a scientist!

Meteorologists measure the weather every day.

They look for **patterns** in the weather.

When meteorologists predict the weather, we call it a weather forecast.

1

Become a meteorologist!

a Collect information about the weather where you live.

b What will you measure?

c How often will you take measurements?

d How will you record your measurements?

e Use your weather chart to record your weather information.

f Change your chart every day to show the day's weather.

g Record your weather measurements every day for about 30 days.

Do you notice any patterns in the weather?

2

a Watch a weather forecast on the internet or television. Talk to a partner about what the weather forecaster says and does. Try to use scientific words.

b Use your measurements of the weather to role-play a weather forecast.

Scientific word
patterns

The seasons

Think like a scientist!

You know about the Sun, rain and wind. Now you will find out about the seasons.

The weather is not the same all over the world. It often depends on the time of year or the season.

The Earth has four seasons. They are winter, spring, summer and autumn.

We wear different clothes in different seasons.

1

Design a page for a calendar.

a Choose a month and decide which season it belongs to.

b Draw a picture to show your month and the season.

c Write a sentence to go with your picture. Describe the season.

What clues can you see to show what season it is? Which season is it where you live?

Extreme weather

Think like a scientist!

Weather can change. Sometimes it can be extreme (very powerful) and dangerous.

A **hurricane** is a big storm with strong winds and lots of rain. It can cause lots of damage.

A **blizzard** happens when there is lots of snow and wind. It is difficult to see, so driving is not safe.

A **monsoon** brings heavy rain, thunderstorms and floods. In some places, like Indonesia, people build houses on stilts (poles) to keep them from flooding.

hurricane winds

houses built on stilts

Weather forecasts help people to prepare for severe (very bad) weather. This way, they can stay safe.

1

Look at the weather forecast.

a How many types of weather does it show? Describe them.

b What clothes should you wear for each type of weather?

c What are the warmest and coolest temperatures?

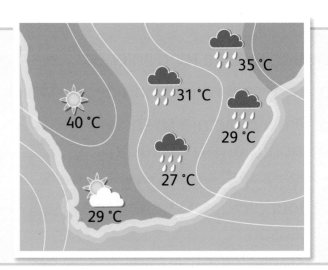

35 °C
31 °C
40 °C
29 °C
27 °C
29 °C

What have you learnt about living things in their environment?

1

Work in a small group.

a Write a quiz that has five questions. The questions should test what learners know about living things in the environment. Make sure that you know the answers.

b Give your quiz to another group to answer.

c How many questions did they get right?

2

a Work with a partner. Pick a part of the world. Make a pretend weather forecast.

b Describe the clothes you would need to wear. Then describe the environment.

c Can others guess where you are?

What can you remember?

You have been learning about living things in their environment. Can you:

✔ name some of the living things around you?

✔ sort living things into groups?

✔ describe what a habitat is?

✔ describe some habitats and say what lives there?

✔ describe one way humans can damage the environment?

✔ say something you can do to help to care for and protect the environment?

✔ say what the weather is like where you live?

Quiz 1: Biology

1 Which of these are living things?

a
b
c
d

e
f

2 Name three things the baby can do that the baby doll cannot.

3 Think about the living things around your school.
   a Write the names of three plants you would find in group 1.
   b Write the names of three animals you would find in group 2.

   (group 1 – plants where I live)   (group 2 – animals where I live)

4 Copy and finish the sentence. Choose one of the three words.
   An animal's home is called its _____.

   (house)   (habitat)   (hole)

5 Where does each animal live?

desert habitat   rainforest habitat

6 Class 2 hunted for invertebrates around school.
   This is their chart.

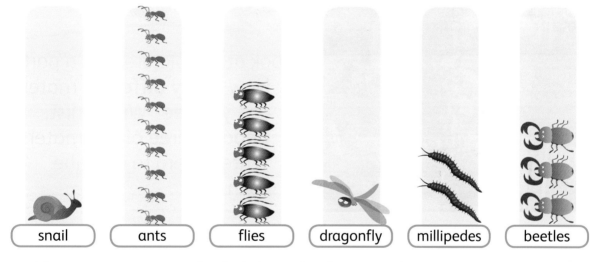

snail   ants   flies   dragonfly   millipedes   beetles

a How many animals did they find in total?
b Which animal did they find the most of?
c Name another invertebrate that they might find.

7 Describe one way you could help to care for your environment.

8 List two pieces of information that you would put in
   a weather forecast.

Unit 2 Material properties

Describing materials

Think like a scientist!

Everything is made from **materials** – all the things we use, our clothes and our toys. We describe materials by how they look and feel. This is called the **property** of the material.

This wooden bowl feels smooth.

Scientific words

materials
property
different
sort
plastic
wood
fabric
compare

Talk partners

Look at the picture with a partner.
a How many **different** materials can you see? Write a list.
b Choose three of the materials. Write a word to describe each one.

1

Class 2 have not put away their toys. Help Mrs Abbas to **sort** the toys by the type of material. The toys are made from **plastic**, **wood** and **fabric**.

a List the toys for each box.

b **Compare** your list with a partner's. Are they the same?

plastic   fabric   wood

Materials in your classroom

1

a Look around your classroom. Find:

- three things made from fabric
- three things made from wood
- three things made from plastic.

b Write a list in a table like this:

Object	Material it is made of ...
pencil case	plastic
chair	wood

Think like a scientist!

Fabrics are made from different types of materials. Cotton, wool, silk and polyester are different types of fabrics.

2

a What other materials do you see in your classroom?

b Add these to your table from Activity 1.

c Share your list with a partner. Did your partner see a material that you did not?

Talk partners

a Can you name a material that is not in the classroom?

b What things are made from that material? Add these to your table from Activity 1.

33

Properties of materials

Scientific word
stone

Think like a scientist!

We can group or sort materials by their properties (how they look or feel). Here are some words to describe materials:

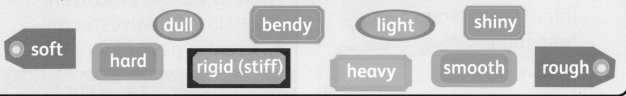

dull   bendy   light   shiny

soft   hard   rigid (stiff)   heavy   smooth   rough

1

a Make your own labels. Use them to label objects (things made from materials) in the classroom.

b Which of your senses have helped you to decide on a label?

2

We can use materials to make many different objects.

a Choose a material from these six words:

glass   leather   metal   **stone**   paper   cotton

b Create a spider diagram. Write the name of your material in the middle of your page.

c Show the uses of the material. Write or draw them around the name.

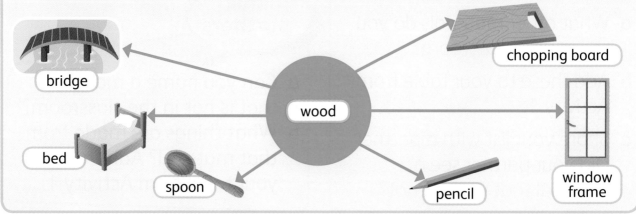

bridge

chopping board

bed

wood

window frame

spoon

pencil

Materials choices

Talk partners

Mr Jumble is not very good at making sensible choices.

His shirt is made of candle wax. His shoes are made of brick. Very silly! Talk to a partner about these questions.

a Why are Mr Jumble's clothes not the right materials?

b Can you think of better materials for a shirt and shoes?

c Why are your choices better?

1

a Draw and label a house for Mr Jumble. Choose silly materials for the roof, windows and walls.

b Write a sentence to explain why the materials are not good choices.

c Write a sentence to explain what materials he should use instead.

2

Play this game with a partner.

a Write the names of different objects and materials on two spinners.

b Use a pencil and paperclip. Spin to find an object, then a material. Which are sensible choices? Why?

c Which choices are silly? Why?

d Swap your game with other pairs and play again.

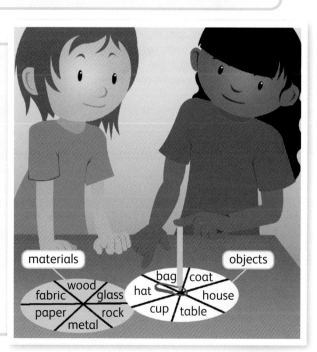

What are rocks?

Think like a scientist!

You will now learn about a special material that is all over the world – rock.

If you dig anywhere, deep enough, you will find rock.

Our **planet** Earth is made from rock.

Rock is under fields and roads, deserts and mountains.

Different rocks have different properties. We use them in different ways.

Is there rock under the ocean?

1

You will need...
• chocolate samples

Work in your group to compare some chocolate rocks!

a Your teacher will give you some chocolate 'rocks'. Do not eat them!

b Write a list of words to describe the rocks. Use these ideas to help you.

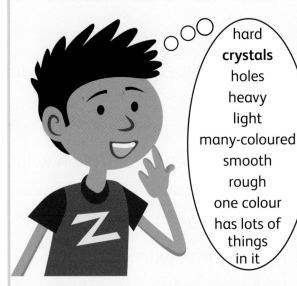

hard
crystals
holes
heavy
light
many-coloured
smooth
rough
one colour
has lots of things in it

c Sort your rocks into groups.

d Show your sorted rocks to another group. Can they guess how you sorted them?

Scientific words
planet
crystals

Space rocks!

Think like a scientist!

Rocks have different colours and **textures** (the way something feels).

Rocks have different names.

Sometimes rocks have crystals in them. We can polish crystals and use them to create jewellery.

Diamond is the hardest rock. Diamonds are difficult to find and very valuable.

diamond

1

You and your group have special jobs. You are **geologists** (scientists who study rocks) on a **space** mission. You will visit a newly-discovered planet.

You will need...
• rocks

a Look at the rocks you bring back to your laboratory (where scientists do experiments).

b Look at each rock. Think of words to describe it. Write them down.

c Draw a detailed picture of each rock. Write down what it looks like from all sides.

d Make sure you think about all the things on this checklist:

- ❒ colour
- ❒ texture
- ❒ marbled (swirly patterns)
- ❒ holes
- ❒ crystals
- ❒ solid

Talk partners

Talk to a partner. Which is your favourite rock so far? Why?

Scientific words

textures
geologists
space

Describing rocks

Scientific words
identify   pebbles

Think like a scientist!

Scientists, called geologists, sort and **identify** or name rocks. They look at the properties of rocks to help them do this.

1

You will need...
- rocks
- hand lens

a Look carefully at some rocks. Use rocks (**pebbles** and stones) that your teacher provides. Or, go outside and find some rocks to look at.

b In your group, talk about how you could group and sort the rocks.

c Study the colour and texture of the surfaces. Are they rough or smooth?

d Look closely through a hand lens. Is the rock the same all the way through?

e Try grouping your rocks. Are there any 'odd ones out'?

Challenge yourself!

Use books or the internet to help you to identify (find out about and name) your rocks.

Talk partners

Play this game with a partner.

a Think of one rock. Ask a partner to guess which rock you are thinking of by asking questions.

b You may only answer 'yes' or 'no'. Your partner must think carefully before asking the questions.

c Can your partner discover your rock in five questions or less?

Is it one colour all the way through?

No.

Using rocks

Think like a scientist!

The properties of different types of rock make them useful for different jobs.

Some colourful rocks are used in jewellery.

Talk partners

Look at this castle. It is made from a hard rock called limestone. Talk to a partner.

Why is limestone a good choice for this building?

Mrs Abbas writes on a board with chalk. Chalk is a very different type of rock. It is special because it is soft and crumbly.

a What property of chalk makes it good for writing?

b Is chalk a good rock to use for building a house? Why?

Challenge yourself!

a Use books or the internet to help you to identify (find out and name) some rocks.

b Can you find any of these rocks where you live?

c Name some things that are made from these rocks.

d Why are these rocks a good choice of material for these things?

Testing rocks

Scientific word
prediction

Think like a scientist!

You know that there are different types of rocks.

You know that materials, including rocks, have certain properties.

Now you will test some rocks to find out which is the hardest.

Hardness is a property of a material.

Talk partners

Talk in your group about how to find out which rock is the hardest.

What evidence can we collect?

How will we keep the test fair?

How do we record what we find?

1

You will need...
- selection of rocks (such as basalt, chalk, sandstone, limestone),
- coin
- cloth

a Choose four different rocks. Label them 1 to 4.

b Scratch each rock with your fingernail. Can you see the scratch marks?

c Scratch each rock with a coin. Can you see the scratch marks?

d Make a **prediction**: which rock is the hardest and which is the softest? Put them in order from hardest to softest.

e Scratch each rock with every other rock.

f Rub your scratches on the rocks with a cloth. Sometimes the marks will disappear.

How will you make sure you scratch each rock in the same way?

Looking at results

1

Class 2 did an investigation to test how hard their rocks were:

Was scratched by:				
	Rock 1	**Rock 2**	**Rock 3**	**Rock 4**
Rock 1		✗	✗	✗
Rock 2	✔		✔	✗
Rock 3	✔	✗		✗
Rock 4	✔	✔	✔	

Record your results from Activity 1 on page 40 in a table like this.

Think like a scientist!

A hard rock marks a softer rock by scratching it.

Friedrich Mohs was a German geologist. He invented a **scale of hardness** called the Mohs scale. It shows that diamond is the hardest rock. No other rock can scratch it.

Talc is the softest kind of rock. All other rocks can scratch it.

Scientific words

scale of hardness

2

The class made a scale of hardness for their rocks.

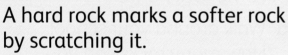

hardest	1	3	2	4	softest

a Look at the table in Activity 1. Which was the hardest rock? It scratched all the other rocks.

b Which was the softest rock? All other rocks scratched it.

c Make a hardness scale for your results. Were your predictions correct?

You could name your hardness scale after yourself!

Rocks are useful

Scientific words
volcano   erupts

Think like a scientist!

We can turn rocks into objects that we need. Some rocks are strong and waterproof. They are used to build the outside of buildings. Some rocks are beautiful. They are used inside.

The Taj Mahal in India is made from marble.

Talk partners

Talk to a partner about these rocks. People have made useful objects from them.

a Talk about how we use these rocks.
   Name each item.
b What words can you think of to describe them?
c What property makes these rocks useful?

1

You and a partner will now become rock hunters!

a Walk around your school. How many rocks can you spot? Are the rocks outside or inside the building?

b Make a list of the rocks you find and what they are used for.

c Which type of rock was used the most?

Did you know?

Pumice is rock that floats! It is made when a **volcano erupts**.

How are rocks made?

Think like a scientist!

All rocks are **natural** materials (found in the environment).

Some rocks were made when the Earth was cooling down millions of years ago.

They were squashed, melted or made at the bottom of the sea.

1

Obsidian, basalt and pumice are three different rocks that come from volcanoes.

obsidian

basalt

pumice

a Look carefully at these rocks. How are they similar? How are they different?

b Write down your observations.

c Find out what pumice is used for.

Challenge yourself!

Look at this picture of Mount Etna. It is a volcano that still erupts. It is still throwing out **molten** (melted) rocks called **lava**.

Mount Etna

Find out about other volcanoes that still erupt.

Scientific words

natural   molten

lava

What is in a rock?

> **Think like a scientist!**

Some rocks contain amazing things. **Fossils** are the remains of plants and animals from millions of years ago.

Plants or animals were trapped in rock while it was forming (being made). In the **process**, the plants or animals turned into rock.

fossil of a fish

> **Scientific words**
> fossils
> process

1

Work in a small group.

The following pictures and sentences describe how fossils form. They are mixed up.

a Use the internet or books to research how fossils formed.

b Match the sentences below (numbered 1 to 4) to the pictures. Put them in the correct order.

A  B  C  D

  1 After death, mud or sand covered some animals.

  2 More bits of rock covered the rotting animals. They were washed down by rivers.

  3 The hard parts of the animals remained. They were squashed and covered by new rock.

  4 After a very long time, the land changed and the animal remains changed to rock. We call these fossils.

More about fossils

1

You are going to make fossils!

You will need...

- plastic container
- modelling clay
- plaster of Paris
- container for mixing the plaster
- water
- leaves
- shells or plastic animals
- paint and paintbrush

- Cover the bottom of a plastic container with about 2 cm of modelling clay.
- Press a few plastic animals, shells or leaves into the clay.
- Remove the objects. You should see the pattern of the object in the clay.
- Mix one-quarter of a cup of plaster of Paris with water until it is quite runny.
- Carefully pour the plaster over the clay. Make a 2–3 cm layer.
- Let the plaster dry overnight.
- When the plaster is dry, carefully take it out of the container.
- You have made your own fossil! Paint it to look more like a real fossil.

Be careful ⚠

Do not breathe in any plaster of Paris powder. It could make you cough.
Do not touch the plaster while it is drying.

Rocks make soils!

Scientific word
soil

Think like a scientist!

Rocks are broken down by rain, wind and water to form **soil**.

Soil is a mixture of tiny ground-down pieces of rock, dead plants, water and air.

Soil can be black, red, yellow or brown. The type and colour of soil depends on the rocks that made it.

1

You will need...
- small bags or cups
- spoon
- hand lens

You are going to be a soil scientist!

a Walk around your school grounds or neighbourhood. Look for different types of soil.

b Use a spoon to take a small sample of soil that is allowed. Put it in a small bag or cup.

c Talk to your group. Look at different samples from different places. Use a hand lens.

d Are all the soils the same?

e What is the same and what is different? Think about colour and texture. Are there stones or parts of plants in your soils?

f Are there any animals in your soils? What kinds of animals? Why do you think they are in the soil?

Be careful ⚠

Always wash your hands after handling soil. Put any animals back where they came from.

Natural or man-made?

Think like a scientist!

Materials come from different **sources** (places or things).

Some materials are **natural**. We find them in nature – such as wood and rock.

Some materials are **man-made**. People make things like plastic and paper.

natural materials

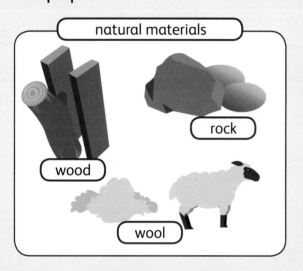

rock

wood

wool

man-made materials

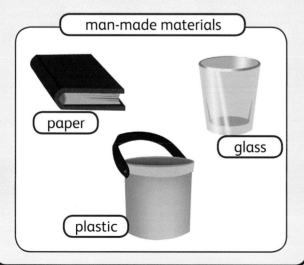

paper

glass

plastic

1

You are going on a materials hunt! Take a small box or bag with you.

a Walk around your school. Look for different materials.

b Do not damage anything. Take a small piece of what is allowed.

c Talk to your group. Which materials look natural? Which are man-made?

d Sort your materials into two groups.

e Record your groups. You could draw two circles like this:

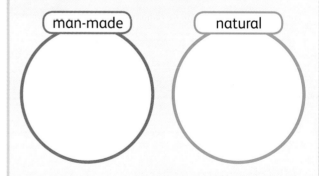

man-made

natural

f Keep your materials. You will look at them again later.

Scientific words

sources

natural

man-made

Natural materials

Think like a scientist!

Sometimes people take a natural material and process it. They change the material so that they can use it.

Wool is a natural material that comes from a sheep.

We change sheep's wool so that we can use it. We wash it and spin it into yarn. We process it.

We use the yarn to knit pullovers or weave woollen cloth.

1

a Do some research. How does a sheep's fleece change into a woollen pullover?

b Draw a flow chart to show the different stages.

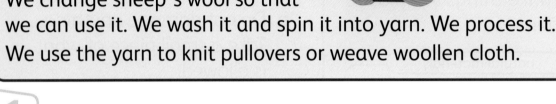

This flow chart shows how to wash your hands.

2

Which materials are natural? Decide how you will record your answers.

Making paper (1)

> ## Think like a scientist!
>
> Paper is a material that we use all the time. It is a processed material.
>
> Paper is made from wood – a natural material. We take natural wood and change it into something different. Then we use it in another way – as paper.
>
> Paper is a material that we can **recycle**. We can use it again.

Scientific word
recycle

Make some recycled paper.
The process will take two days.

You will need...
- five sheets of paper towels or soft paper (or newspaper)
- scissors
- bowl or bucket
- warm water
- wooden spoon

- Cut your old paper into tiny pieces. Paper towels or soft paper are best.

- Put your paper pieces in a bowl or bucket. Cover them with warm water.

- Mix until the paper is very wet.

- Stir the mixture. Leave the paper pieces for a few hours or overnight.

Making paper (2)

1

You left your paper pulp overnight. Now finish the process.

You will need...

- tablespoon
- sieve
- sharp pencil
- cornflour
- kitchen strainer
- sheets of newspaper
- tap water
- aluminium foil
- rolling pin or bottle
- blender (optional)

- Add a few tablespoons of cornflour. Add a little tap water. Mix it.

- If you have a blender, your teacher can blend the paper into a pulp (a watery mess). Or, rub it through a sieve.

- Put your paper pulp into a kitchen strainer. Let all the water drip through.

- Take a piece of aluminium foil. Use the size of the paper you want to make. Punch holes in it with a sharp pencil.

- Put your foil on top of some sheets of newspaper.

- Spoon your pulp onto the foil. Press it to the shape you want. Squeeze out as much water as you can. Roll a rolling pin or bottle across the pulp to squeeze out more water.

- Leave your paper to dry.

- Congratulations! You have processed a natural material.

Now you can use your recycled hand-made paper.

Processing natural materials

Think like a scientist!

Silk is another natural material. Silkworms are animals that make silk thread. Humans process the silk thread to make silk cloth.

silk cloth

Scientific word
cocoons

1

These pictures show how natural silk is processed (made into silk cloth).

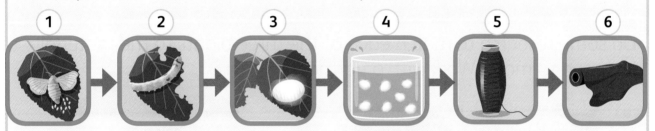

The pictures are in the right order but the sentences are mixed up.
Put the sentences in the right order and match them to the pictures.

a They spin **cocoons**.

b The eggs hatch and the larvae feed on mulberry leaves.

c The cocoons are steamed and washed.

d The cloth is made.

e The threads are wound together.

f A silk moth lays eggs.

2

Look back at the circle diagram you made in Activity 1 on page 47.

a Think about what you know now. Are some materials in the wrong group?

b Change any materials that are in the wrong group.

c What made you decide which group to choose for your materials?

Materials from plants

Think like a scientist!

Some of the natural materials we use come from plants.

You might know that wood comes from trees. Did you know that we use materials from plants in many different ways?

1

Do some research to match each of the three plants to the material it is used to make. Work with a partner.

a

b

c

coir mat

cotton shirt

rubber gloves

2

a Look around your school or home. Make a list of materials you think come from plants. How are these materials used?

b Compare your list with your partner's list. Check with your teacher if you are unsure about any material.

c How many did you find?

Scientific words

coir

rubber

Painting from plants

marigold flower | turmeric root

henna plant

These patterns are made from the powdered leaves of a henna plant.

Think like a scientist!

We use plants to make medicines, building materials, clothes and for fuel. We also eat plants!

Artists have used plants to make paints since very long ago. Flowers such as marigolds, and roots such as turmeric give strong natural colours.

1

Paint with plants.

a Ask an adult to slice the red cabbage and turmeric root. Leave them to soak for an hour in separate bowls of warm water.

b Use the pale purple cabbage water to paint all over your sheet of paper. Paint a design on this using lemon juice. Wow! It changes colour!

c Now use the yellow turmeric water to paint on another sheet of paper. What happens when you add liquid soap?

d Experiment with other plants. Can you make colours from them?

You will need...
- red cabbage
- turmeric root
- two bowls of warm water
- paper
- paintbrush
- lemon juice
- liquid soap
- other plants

Metal is a natural material

> **Think like a scientist!**

Scientific words
ores   smelting

smelting ores

You now know a lot about natural materials and rocks. But did you know that metal is a natural material that is found in rocks?

All sorts of metals come from inside special rocks called **ores**.

The ores are crushed and heated to get out the metal.

1

You will need...
- old magazines or catalogues
- scissors
- glue
- large sheet of paper

Metal is one of our most useful materials.

a Work with a partner. Make a collage of pictures of objects made from metal. Cut out pictures from old magazines or catalogues. Stick them onto a large sheet of paper.

b Add the names of different metals to your picture.

c How many metals can you name?

2

Gold is a very precious metal. It can be found in rocks but also sometimes in streams and rivers.

gold nugget

Do some research to make a fact file about gold.

> **Talk partners**

Find out about the story of King Midas. In the story, everything the king touched turned to gold. Talk to a partner about the story.

What have you learnt about material properties?

1

Play a game about materials in small teams.

- Your teacher will put up posters showing different types of materials such as fabric, rock and metal.

- The first person in the team should go to the front of the class. Collect the name of a material, such as cotton.

- The team will discuss which group the material belongs to.

- Your teacher will say 'Go'. The first person must run and stand next to the poster where the material fits best.

- Every correct answer scores a point.

- For the next question, change the runner.

- The team with the most points wins!

2

Malia is not sure about the differences between natural, man-made or processed materials. Write a note to her to describe the differences.

What can you remember?

You have been learning about materials. Can you:

✔ name some different rocks?

✔ describe the properties of some rocks?

✔ name some objects that can be made from rocks?

✔ describe some materials?

✔ name some natural materials?

✔ name some man-made materials?

Unit 3 Material changes

What are materials?

Think like a scientist!

The word **material** describes what things are made from. Materials have **properties** (they behave in particular ways) that make them useful for **different** jobs.

Scientific words

material   properties   different
transparent opaque

Talk partners

Materials can be soft, hard, stiff, bendy, waterproof, absorbent, **transparent** or **opaque**. These are all properties of materials. Talk to a partner. How many other properties can you think of?

1

Make a materials cube.

wood

plastic paper metal

glass

fabric

- Cut out the net of a cube.
- Write the names of six materials on the net.
- Make the cube. Throw it on a table.

a Write down the material name that is on the top. Challenge your group to find objects made from that material in the classroom.

b Write them in a list.

c Talk about why the material is a good choice for the objects. Throw your cube again.

Changing materials

Think like a scientist!

We can change some materials. We can squash, bend, twist or stretch them. Then the materials can change back!

When a material can change back to the way it was, the change is **reversible**.

You will need...
- modelling dough

1

a Take a ball of modelling dough. Squash it. Bend it. Twist it. Stretch it.

b Roll your dough back into a ball after each change. You are changing it back to the shape you started with. This is a reversible change.

Did you know?

Bubble gum is very stretchy. The record for the biggest bubble gum bubble is 50.8 cm.

2

Use your dough from Activity 1. The challenge is to make a bird.

a Take turns to choose a number (from 1 to 6) from a bag.
Do what the number says:

1 – squash your dough

2 – bend your dough

3 – twist your dough

4 – stretch your dough

5 or 6 – choose how to change it.

b Who will be first to make a bird?

Reversible changes

Talk partners

Talk to a partner about these materials.

a Which can you bend?
b Which can you squash?
c Which can you twist?
d Which can you stretch?
e Can you change back the material to the way it was? Is the change reversible or not?

elastic bands

corrugated cardboard

T-shirt

can

bread dough

wood

balloon

1

Try this:

- Stand up.
- Very gently, bend part of your body. You could bend your arm or your leg.
- Now twist part of your body.
- Now stretch your body.
- Very gently, squash part of your body such as your arm, leg or face. Take care.

a Are these changes to your body shape reversible or not?

b What would happen if you could not reverse these changes?

Heating materials

Think like a scientist!

You know that the shapes of some materials can be changed. These are reversible changes. The materials change back to the way they were. Some changes are **irreversible**. This means they cannot be changed back. Many foods that we eat change when we **heat** them. These are irreversible changes, for example, a baked cake or a cooked egg.

a cake that is baking

1

a Make a list of your favourite foods.

b Circle those that have been cooked (such as bread or chicken).

c Can the change from raw (uncooked) to cooked be reversed? Or, is it an irreversible change?

Scientific words

irreversible
heat
predict
melt
solid
liquid

2

Work in a small group.

a Talk about what you think will happen to these foods when they are heated.

ice cube

tomato

chocolate

butter

raw egg

b **Predict** which foods will **melt** (change from **solid** to **liquid**) when heated.

c List the foods that you predicted will melt in hot sun.

59

⟳ Testing ideas

1

a Test your foods to see if they change when heated. Put a small amount of the food in a thin foil tray over a bowl of hot water.

Be careful ⚠

Be very careful – hot water can burn you.

You will need...
- aluminium foil
- selection of foods to test
- bowl of hot water
- tongs or a clothes peg to remove the aluminium tray from the water safely

b Write your results in a table like this.

Food	What it looked like when cold	What it looked like when warmed	Changed or not?
butter	*yellow block*	*clear yellow liquid*	*yes, melted*
bread	*white, soft with holes*	*same*	*no*
ice			
chocolate			

c Were your predictions correct?

d Which changes are reversible or irreversible?

e Talk to your group. How could you test whether the melted materials could change back from liquids (runny) to solids (keep their shape)?

f Try your ideas. What happened?

Solids and liquids

Think like a scientist!

Scientific word
solidifies   freezes

Chocolate can change to runny liquid when it is heated. It becomes hard again when it is put in a fridge. It becomes a solid. It **solidifies**. Ice can turn to liquid water when it is heated. Water needs to be put in a very cold freezer to turn back to solid ice. It **freezes**.

1

You will need...
- liquids
- plastic cups
- freezer

a Try freezing liquids such as milk or fruit juice. Pour some liquid into a plastic cup. Place it in the freezer overnight.

b What do you think it will look like?

c Do all liquids freeze? How could you find out?

d Make a table of your predictions and results.

How can you keep your tests fair?

Liquid	What it looks like	My prediction. What will it look like after a night in the freezer?	Did it freeze?
water	*clear, colourless liquid*	*solid block of clear ice*	*yes*

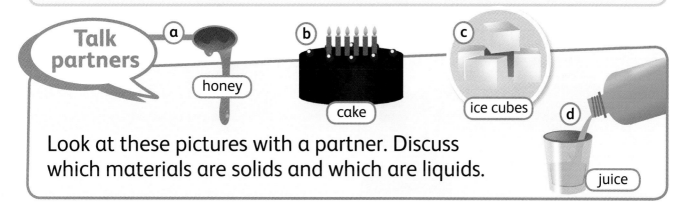

Talk partners

a honey

b cake

c ice cubes

d juice

Look at these pictures with a partner. Discuss which materials are solids and which are liquids.

Solids, liquids and gases

Think like a scientist!

When a solid is heated, it can turn into a liquid.

Scientific words
record
gas

1

You will need...
- three blown-up balloons (balloon A filled with air, balloon B filled with water, balloon C filled with water and frozen)
- freezer

A

B

C

a Work in a group. Hold the balloons. Discuss what they feel like. What is similar and what is different about them?

b Predict what will happen if you leave the balloons in a warm place.

c Decide how you will **record** what you found out.

Will you make a table, a drawing or will you write sentences? Why?

2

The material inside balloon A in Activity 1 is a **gas**. It is not a solid or a liquid. Do you know the names of any gases?

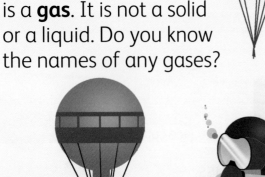

d Write about or draw what you found out.

Changing ice

Talk partners

Talk in a small group. What happens to the weight (mass) of ice when it melts? Do you think it will get heavier, lighter or stay the same?

You will need...
- ice
- clear plastic bags
- kitchen scales or a digital scale
- freezer

a Put some ice cubes in a clear plastic bag.

b Use a kitchen scale or a digital scale to measure how heavy the ice is. Record the weight.

	Ice	Melted ice (water)	Refrozen ice
weight			

c Leave the ice on the scales in a warm place. It will melt and turn to water.

d What do you think will happen to the weight of the ice? Record the weight of the melted ice (water).

e Carefully put your bag of water into the freezer. Leave it overnight.

f Will the refrozen water be heavier, lighter or the same weight? Use a scale to measure how heavy the refrozen water is.

g What have you found out about the weight of ice? Think about the weight when it is frozen, melted and refrozen.

h Why do you think this is?

⟳ How hot?

Think like a scientist!

metal being melted

You know that ice turns to water when it is heated. It can even melt in your hand!

At a very high **temperature**, much hotter than an oven, metal can melt and change to liquid. When it **cools**, it becomes solid again.

Scientific words

temperature
cools
observed

1

Look at these materials and the temperatures needed to melt them.

sugar 185 °C

water 0 °C

chocolate 34 °C

aluminium 660 °C

beeswax 64 °C

a Order them from 'needs least heat to melt' to 'needs most heat to melt'.

b Which material needs the most heat to melt?

2

Rania wondered which material melted fastest. She put a piece of wax crayon, a piece of cheese and some butter in plastic bags. Then she put them in hot water.

a She changed the materials. What must she keep the same to make the test fair?

She **observed** what happened.

b What do you predict happened? Try the investigation yourself.

c Could you improve on Rania's method (way of doing the investigation)?

Warming chocolate

Think like a scientist!

You know that materials can change when heated. Materials can also change when they are cooled.

Chocolate is a very interesting material. It has a special property.

It melts in your mouth at the same temperature as your body.

Challenge yourself!

Find out what the human body temperature is.

Scientific word
process

1

You will need...
- chocolate chips
- clear plastic sandwich bag
- teaspoon
- greaseproof paper
- fridge

Investigate what happens when you warm chocolate.

a Put some chocolate chips in a plastic bag. Hold the bag in both hands.

b Record what happens to the chocolate. Take some photographs or make a drawing. Also write a sentence to describe what happened.

c Are the chocolate chips the same when they are warm as they were before?

d What do we call this **process** (the steps you have taken)?

Cooling chocolate

1

Now reverse the process you investigated on page 65. This means, do it from back to front.

a Put some melted chocolate on a spoon and make little button shapes on greaseproof paper.

b Put the melted chocolate shapes into the sandwich bag, then into the fridge to cool. Predict what will happen.

c After an hour, take the chocolate out of the fridge. What has happened? Was this what you expected?

d What do we call this process?

e Draw a flow chart of what you investigated. Use scientific words to describe the changes you observed.

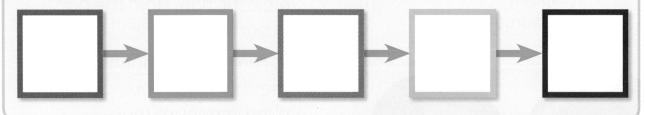

You will need...

• chocolate chips, melted
• teaspoon
• greaseproof paper
• clear plastic sandwich bag
• fridge

Do all types of chocolate melt and solidify in the same way? How can you find out?

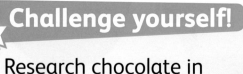

Challenge yourself!

Research chocolate in books and on the internet. What can you find out?

Really hot or not?

Think like a scientist!

Some materials need lots of heat to change from solid to liquid.

Solid metal usually needs to be very hot before it changes to a liquid.

Metal is a good material for making cooking pots. It can get very hot on the fire but not hot enough to melt.

a cast iron cooking pot

1

olive oil
coconut oil
honey
ghee
milk

You will need...
- liquids
- fridge-freezer

Paulo is investigating how materials change. He wants to know which materials are liquid at room temperature. Carry out your own investigation.

a Work as a group to plan your investigation. What will you do?

b Record the room temperature of the air in your classroom.

c Investigate which materials are liquid at room temperature.

d Put your liquids in the fridge and record what happens. What temperature is the inside of the fridge?

e Now put your liquids in the freezer and record what happens. What temperature is the inside of the freezer?

f Record your results.

g Tell another group what you have discovered.

No changing back

Think like a scientist!

As you know, heating can change materials.

Most cooked foods cannot change back to the way they were.

A cooked egg cannot change back to a raw (uncooked) egg. The change is irreversible.

Cakes are made from butter, sugar, eggs and flour.

Mixed together and heated, they make a new material.

Imagine cooking each cake ingredient separately. Then mix them together. Would you get the same result?

1

This potter is making a pot from clay.

You will need...
- clay
- oven

When soft clay is heated it changes. It becomes hard. The clay cannot be made soft again. The change is irreversible.

a Take some modelling clay that can be heated in an oven. Make your own pot.

b Describe the clay before you model it.

c Describe your pot when it comes out of the oven. How has it changed?

Be careful

Do not touch your pot until it has cooled.

Let's cook!

1

Make some chocolate crispy cakes. Use this recipe to help you.

You will need...
- 225 g chocolate
- 125 g breakfast cereal (puffed rice or corn flakes)
- kitchen scale or digital scale
- three tablespoons of golden syrup
- mixing bowl
- spoon
- cooker or microwave oven
- handful of marshmallows or dried fruits (optional)
- paper cake cases
- fridge

- Use a scale to measure your ingredients.
- An adult will help you to melt some chocolate until it becomes runny.
- Add the syrup and breakfast cereal and stir.
- Stir until everything is covered in the chocolate.
- Add marshmallows or dried fruit, if you like. Stir again.

- Put spoonfuls of the mixture into paper cases.
- Put the cakes somewhere cool so the chocolate can solidify.
- Your cakes are ready to eat!

Which ingredients change when heated?

Which ingredients change when cooled?

2

Draw and label a flow chart showing how you made your cakes. Use scientific words to describe how the ingredients have changed.

Disappearing and dissolving

Think like a scientist!

Some materials change when we add them to water. It often looks as if they have disappeared. We say that these materials **dissolve**.

Scientific word
dissolve

1

You will need...
- clear cups, water, spoon, uncooked rice, salt

- Fill half of a clear cup with cold water.
- Drop a small spoonful of rice into the water. Stir the water.

a What do you notice?
The rice has not changed or disappeared. It is the same. It does not dissolve.

- Fill another clear cup halfway with cold water. Add a teaspoon of salt into the water and stir.

b What do you notice now? Has the salt dissolved?

c Taste a drop of the liquid. Can you taste the salt? We cannot see it in the water but it is still there. The salt has dissolved in the water.

2

You will need...
- clear cup, water, teaspoon, salt

a Kalem wondered how much salt could dissolve in water.

b In your group, plan and do an investigation to find out.

c Share your results with another group.

Be careful !

Do not drink this salty water.

SALT

Let's investigate!

1

Frieda wondered if all materials such as salt dissolve in water. She predicted what she thought would happen. Then she did her test. She put a small spoonful of each material into a clear cup of water and stirred. Frieda recorded what each cup of water looked like.

a Work in a group. Repeat (do again) Frieda's test.

b What will you do to keep your test fair? Change the material each time. What will you keep the same each time? Write them in a list.

c Look at Frieda's table below. Copy it and fill it in for your tests. One row has been done for you. Add some other materials to test.

You will need...
- materials (see the table below)
- cups
- spoon
- water

Material	Prediction of what will happen in water	Add cold water	What water looked like	Did it dissolve?
white sugar	*we think it will dissolve but can be tasted in the water*	*needs to be stirred to make it dissolve*	*clear*	*yes*
wheat flour				
brown sugar				
salt				
pepper				

More about dissolving

You will need...

- selection of different sugars: white sugar, brown granulated sugar, dark molasses sugar or muscovado sugar, coloured granulated sugar (if available)
- spoons
- clear cups
- water

a Describe your sugars. Predict what you think will happen when you add the different sugars to water.

b Add a spoon of each sugar to a separate clear cup of cold water. What do you notice?

c Was your prediction correct?

d Did each of the different sugars dissolve? How?

e Do different sugars dissolve in the same way?

Be careful ⚠️

Do not use sweets with nuts.

You will need...

- colourful sugar-coated sweets
- white plate
- water
- camera (optional)

a Arrange the sweets on a white plate. Leave space between each sweet.

b Carefully pour water on the plate to cover it. Try not to disturb the sweets.

c Notice what happens.

d Talk to a partner about what you see. Why do you think this is happening?

e Take a photograph of the pattern or draw it.

f Write a sentence using scientific words to describe what has happened.

Dissolving in other liquids

Think like a scientist!

Materials can dissolve in water and other liquids.

1

You will need...
- selection of liquids (such as water, cooking oil, soda water, lemon juice, white vinegar, shampoo)
- salt
- clear plastic cups
- spoons

a Talk to a partner. Does salt dissolve in other liquids?

b Plan an investigation to find the answer.

c How will you know if the salt has dissolved?

d What will you need to keep the same to make the investigation fair? What will you change?

e Do your investigation.

f Tell your class what you have found out.

2

Investigate whether an egg can dissolve.

You will need...
- raw eggs
- water
- clear cups
- white vinegar

- Take two raw eggs. Notice what they look and feel like.

- Carefully put one egg in a glass of clear water.

- Put the other egg in a glass of white vinegar.

- Leave them both for a week or longer.

- Keep topping up the liquids.

- After a week, remove the eggs.

- What has happened? Wow! A bouncy egg!

Be careful ⚠️

Always wash your hands after touching raw eggs.

⟳ What have you learnt about material changes?

Talk partners

Raj cannot remember the difference between melting and dissolving. Think of a way to help him remember.

melt?

dissolve?

1

Preti the penguin is trapped in the ice.

What is the quickest way to get Preti out without hurting her? Think about how materials can change. What will you do to get Preti out? Why?

What can you remember?

You have been learning about materials and how they can change. Can you:

✔ describe how some materials such as modelling dough can be changed?

✔ say what you need to do to ice to change it to water?

✔ name a change that can be reversed?

✔ name a change that cannot be changed back?

✔ say what sort of change happens when chocolate is melted and then changes back to a solid in a cool place?

✔ describe what happens when we add salt to water and stir?

Quiz 2: Chemistry

1. Look at the objects. They are made from different materials.
   a. Name one that will bend.
   b. Name one that will stretch.
   c. Name one that will squash.

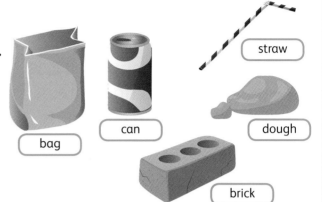

straw

can

dough

bag

brick

2. Glass is a material. Which words from the box describe glass?

   (hard) (bendy) (soft) (opaque) (brittle) (waterproof)

3. Rock is a natural material. Name another natural material.

4. Name two ways we can use rocks.

5. Amina put some white powder into a glass of water.
   She stirred it. It disappeared.
   Copy and complete the sentence. Choose the correct word.

   (melted)   (dissolved)   (frozen)

   The powder had _____.

6. Which of these materials are man-made?
   a. nylon   b. clay   c. wool
   d. plastic   e. metal

7. Plastic is often used to make toys for babies. Name two properties that make it a good material to use.

8   Copy the sentences. Fill in the gaps with the correct words.

reversible   dissolves   irreversible   solidifies   melts

When we heat chocolate, it _____.
When we cool chocolate, it _____.
We say that the change is _____ because it can be
changed back.

9   Choose which materials the objects are made from.
Use the words to help you.

plastic   glass   leather   wood   gold   rubber   cotton

a

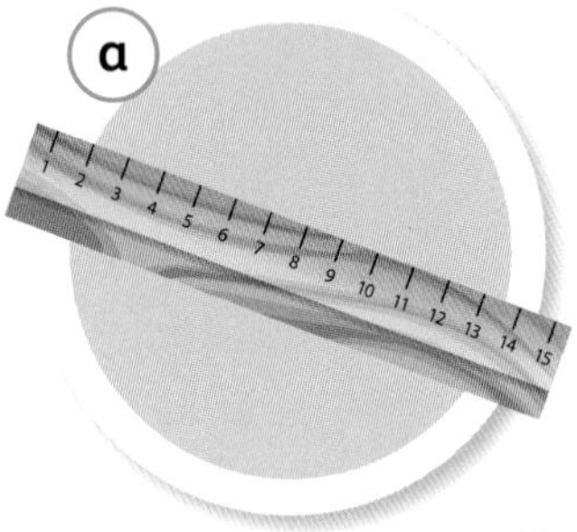

b

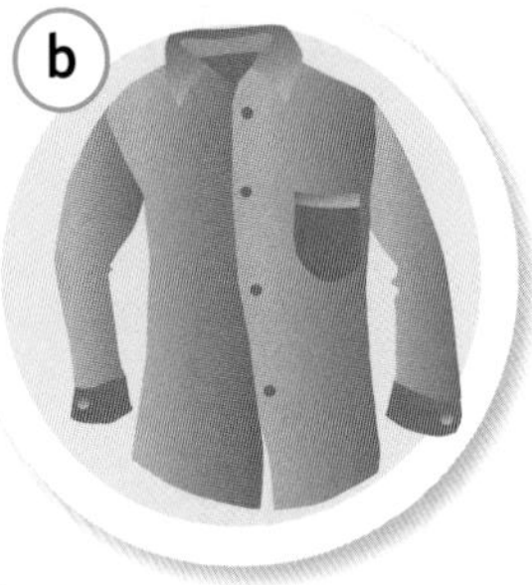

c

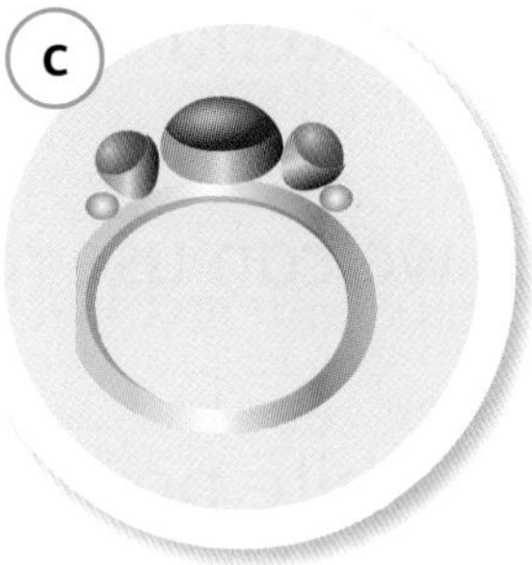

d

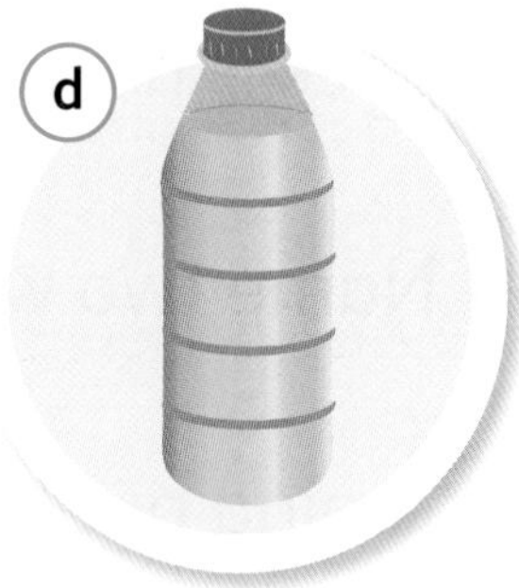

e

f

g

10   Describe what must be done to water to change it to ice.
Choose the correct word.

cool   freeze   heat   irreversible   melt

Water needs to _____ to turn it to ice.

Unit 4 Light and dark

⏻ Seeing light

Think like a scientist!

We need **light** to see. When there is no light, we say it is **dark**.

Talk partners

Talk to a partner.

a Look around. Is it daytime? Is it light or dark outside? Are lights on in the classroom? How can you see things in the classroom?

b Look at the pictures. Does the room look **different** in the dark?

1

a In a small group, talk about light and dark places.

b Make a table of light and dark places. You could do something similar to this:

Light places	Dark places
outside on a sunny day	in a cinema
in my classroom	under the bed
the swimming pool	

c Look at your list of dark places. How could you make them light?

Talk partners

Talk to a partner. Discuss when you have been in the dark. How did it feel? Did you enjoy it? Do you prefer being in the light? Why?

Too many lights?

Think like a scientist!

Scientific words

absence

stars

space

If you live in a large town or city, you may not experience (feel) real darkness.

In towns and cities, so many lights are left on that it is never completely dark.

Darkness is the **absence** of light. There is no light.

In most cities, lights burn brightly all night. We cannot see the **stars** clearly.

1

The photograph shows the Earth at night – from **space**. Look at all the lights!

a Where are the most lights? Why do you think this is?

b Where are the fewest lights?

c Do you see a difference between land and water? Why are there no lights in the oceans? Try to use this scientific word – absence.

Make a dark den

Think like a scientist!

It can be difficult to find a dark place. In a dark place there is no light. We say that darkness is the absence (lack) of light.

1

Make a 'dark den'.

- Find an unused table. It must be big enough for you to sit under.
- Cover the table with a large blanket, curtain or thick cloth. The fabric must be able to touch the floor.
- Make sure there are no gaps (spaces) where the light can get in.
- Sit in your den. Is any light coming in?
- If you see strips of light, add more fabric to cover the gaps.

You will need...
- table
- large blanket, curtain or thick cloth

a You are sitting in the dark. What can you see? Can you see your hand in front of you?

b What could you use to help you to see in your dark den?

Sources of light

Think like a scientist!

Light comes from a **source** – from somewhere. It has a starting point.

A light source is something that makes its own light. There are many different light sources, for example, a torch, a bonfire or a lamp.

The most important source of light is the **Sun**.

Light from the Sun travels super-fast, but it still takes eight minutes to reach the Earth!

the Sun, shining in the sky

Talk partners

Talk to a partner. Light comes from many sources. How many things that make light can you think of? Write them in a list.

1

a Look at the pictures. Which objects are sources of light?

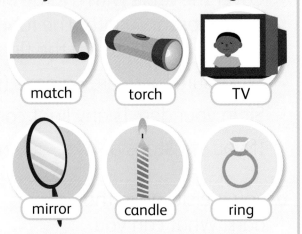

match   torch   TV

mirror   candle   ring

Hint: Imagine having these objects in your dark den. Which objects would make light? Which could you see in the dark?

b Discuss the objects that are not light sources. Why not?

Scientific words

source
Sun

Brightness

Think like a scientist!

The **brightness** (strength) of light sources changes.
Some are brighter than others.
Very **bright** (strong) light sources include the Sun and floodlights in a sports stadium.

Some sources of light are weak. A nightlight has a **dim** light.

The Sun is the brightest light source. We need to protect our bodies from burning in the Sun. We can stay in the shade or use sun lotion.

1 Write some instructions for younger learners. Teach them how to stay safe in the Sun.

2 These pictures show sources of light.

a — Sun

b — kitchen light

c — car headlight

d — floodlight

e — small torch

f — candle

Put them in order from brightest to dimmest.

Scientific words

brightness
bright
dim

You will need...
• two torches

3

a Look at two torches. Which is the brightest – and dimmest?

b Use the torches in your dark den. Which is brighter?

81

Dim or bright?

Think like a scientist!

Some sources of light are dim. They are not very bright.

Matches, candles or small torches may give dim light.

Lamps are sources of light in many homes.

Some lamps give a dimmer light than others.

Talk partners

Talk to a partner. List the light sources in your school.
a Which is the dimmest? Which is the brightest?
b When would you need a very bright light?
c When would you want a light to be dim?

1

In a group, play a game of charades – an action game with no words.

a Choose a light source. Mime it to your group. Use actions but no words to describe it.

b Can the rest of the group guess the light source?

Did you know?

The world's brightest torch can light objects that are up to 14 kilometres away. This torch is as bright as 52 million candles!

⟳ Reflecting light

Think like a scientist!

Some things **reflect** light. They do not make their own light.

Light from a light source bounces off the object. It appears to be bright.

We can see reflective materials in the dark when light bounces off them.

We can see the Moon at night because it reflects light.

the Moon

safety clothing with strips of reflective material

Scientific words
reflect   predict
compare

1

Look at these objects.

a **Predict** which objects will reflect light and which will not.

b List the two groups of objects. Add more if you can. Label one group 'reflects light' and the second group 'does not reflect light'.

c **Compare** your list with a partner's. Are they the same?

d Talk to a partner about how you might test your ideas.

Talk partners

Ade has a new bicycle. Talk to your partner.
a Why does Ade need a light on the front of his bike?
b Why does he have a reflector on the back of his bike?

Shiny surfaces

Think like a scientist!

You have found out that some objects and materials reflect light really well. Not all objects reflect light.

Scientific words

reflection
shiny

1

You will need...

- aluminium foil
- mirror
- collection of shiny and dull materials

a Look in the mirror. Can you see your **reflection** (your face in the mirror)?

b Look at the **shiny** side of the foil. Can you see your reflection?

c Crush the foil; then smooth it out. You are making the surface bumpy and dull.

d Look at your reflection in the crushed foil. What has happened?

e Try to see your reflection in other places. Use different materials, shiny and dull, to test if you can see your reflection.

f Think of objects in which you can see your reflection. What do they have in common?

2

Look around your school for shiny surfaces and smooth objects.

a Can you see your reflection in the surfaces? Make a list.

b Do shiny and smooth objects make the best reflectors?

Investigating materials

Think like a scientist!

You know what a light source is. You also know that some materials reflect light from a source.

1

Make an armband that you can see in dim light.

You will need...
- selection of different-coloured fabrics and papers
- dark den
- torch
- scissors
- card
- glue and safety pin for badge

a Why might people want to be seen in dim light?
Hint: Think about traffic.

b Work in a group. Investigate your materials. Predict which ones will be easy to see in dim light. Which ones will not?

c Look at the materials in your dark den (from page 79). Can you see the materials in the dark? Now look at them with a torch.

d Test each material in your dark den. Which ones can you see best in dim light?

e Share your ideas with other groups.

f Make an armband from the best (most reflective) material. It will help car drivers to spot you when it gets dark.

Light from animals

Think like a scientist!

Some animals live in very dark places. They can make their own light.

Look at the Japanese lamp. What is making the light?

The lamp is full of amazing insects called fireflies. They have tails that light up! Imagine if you could do that!

Other living things can make their own light. They use their bodies. Look at the angler fish. It lives deep in the ocean where there is no light. The angler fish uses its light to attract food.

Japanese lamp

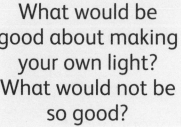
firefly

angler fish

Talk partners

Talk to a partner. Imagine having a light at the end of your finger! What could you do?

What would be good about making your own light? What would not be so good?

1

a Decorate your dark den from page 79 with glowing animals.

b Use glow-in-the-dark paint or plastic shapes to make them.

More light makers and reflectors

Think like a scientist!

These mushrooms, from Brazil, can make their own light. They glow in the dark!

glow-in-the-dark mushrooms

Some animals appear to make light. Look at the lemur's eyes. They appear to glow. Yet its eyes are only reflecting the light that shines on them.

lemur

Scientific word
bioluminescence

1

Do you remember the light sources on page 80? Some objects were there to trick you. The mirror and the diamond ring reflect the light that shines on them.

In a group, walk around the school. Make a table with two columns, as shown below.

a List all the light sources you can find in one column.

b In the other column, list all the light reflectors you can find.

Light sources	Light reflectors
overhead lights	mirror
torch	

Challenge yourself!

The word for light made by living things is **bioluminescence** (say *bi – o – loom – in – ess – ense*).

Try to remember this scientific word.

Nocturnal animals

Think like a scientist!

You know that it is dark at night. Did you know that some animals like the dark more than the day? These are **nocturnal** animals. They wake up when we go to bed.
Look at these nocturnal animals.

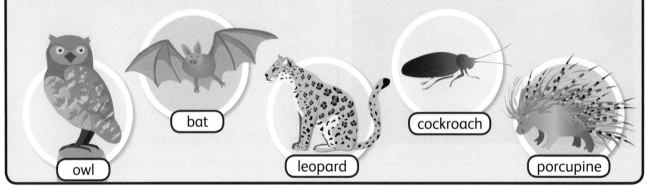

bat

cockroach

owl

leopard

porcupine

1

a Do some research about the nocturnal animals where you live.

b Make a nocturnal display in your classroom.

Do animals that like to live in daylight have a special name?

Scientific word
nocturnal

Talk partners

Talk to a partner.

a Imagine if humans were nocturnal. We would wake up at night and go to sleep during the day.

b What would be good about that? What would not be good about it?

c Many people have to work all night. Think of hospital workers, drivers and police. Would you like that? Why or why not?

Travelling light

Think like a scientist!

You know that light reflects, or bounces off some materials. Now you will learn how light moves.

Light travels (moves) from a light source in straight lines. It cannot bend around objects or corners.

Sometimes you can see straight lines of light through trees or clouds. These lines are called **light rays**.

light rays through trees

Scientific words
light rays

1

You will need...
• cardboard tube • torch

a Look through a cardboard tube at a light source. Can you see light at the end of the tube?

b Now bend the tube. Can you see light?

c Light cannot move around the bend in the tube, so you cannot see any light. Describe what is happening. Use the scientific word.

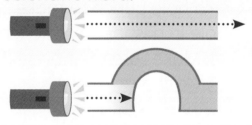

2

You will need...
• 'dark den' • torch • hair comb

a Go inside your dark den (from page 79).

b Shine a torch through a comb.

c Can you see the straight lines of light (light rays)? They should come through the gaps in the comb. The light rays are travelling in straight lines.

Investigating how light travels

Think like a scientist!

Light travels from a source in straight lines. It cannot move around corners.

1

You will need...
- hole punch
- cardboard shoebox
- marker pen
- ruler
- torch

a Work with a partner. Use a hole punch to make a hole in a shoebox at each end. Make sure the holes are in a line.

b Shine the torch beam through the holes. Can you see the light ray (straight line of light)?

c Talk to a partner about what you see. Why do you think this happens?

2

Learn this rhyme with a partner. It will help you to remember how light travels:

Ray of light

Ray of light

In the day or in the night

Light goes travelling as it shines

It only travels in straight lines.

3

Make a mini-book of what you know about light.

You could make it in the shape of a torch. Include illustrations.

Using light

Think like a scientist!

We need light to see. We use light to help us see when it is dark.

We use light in other ways.

Here is a code (secret message) called Morse code. Sailors use it to signal messages. They send a message using short and long flashes of light. A dash (line) means 'leave on the light for one to two seconds'. A dot means 'flash the light quickly'.

A	•▬	J	•▬▬▬	S	•••
B	▬•••	K	▬•▬	T	▬
C	▬•▬•	L	•▬••	U	••▬
D	▬••	M	▬▬	V	•••▬
E	•	N	▬•	W	•▬▬
F	••▬•	O	▬▬▬	X	▬••▬
G	▬▬•	P	•▬▬•	Y	▬•▬▬
H	••••	Q	▬▬•▬	Z	▬▬••
I	••	R	•▬•		

Morse code

You will need...
- torch

1

a Use a torch to practise sending a Morse code SOS message. SOS means that you need help.

b Send a different short message. Can the group understand your message?

Talk partners

Light is important in some festivals and celebrations.

a Talk to your partner about a festival you know. Draw a picture.

A

Light is used to warn people of danger.

b Look at pictures A and B. Talk about what the lights are used for.

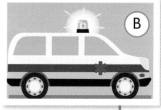
B

c Draw two other lights that help us to stay safe.

Identifying shadows

Think like a scientist!

You know that darkness is the absence (lack) of light. When there is no light, it is dark.

Some materials block light. They stop light from coming through. Objects that are blocking light make **shadows**. Shadows are similar to the objects that made them.

Scientific word
shadows

2

Look at these shadows. What objects made them? Write the name of each object.

a

b

c

d

You will need...
• torch

1

a Shine a torch onto a wall. Can you see the light on the wall?

b Now put your hand in front of the torch. Can you see the light on the wall? Is some of the light blocked? Your hand stopped the light from reaching the wall.

When we block the path of light, a shadow forms.

You will need...
• torch

3

a Choose an object that you see in your classroom.

b Use a torch to make the shadow of the object.

c Draw the shape of the shadow.

d Ask a partner to guess the object from the shape you drew.

Shadows outdoors

Think like a scientist!

You know that the Sun is a source of light. When light is blocked, it makes shadows.

1

a Go outside on a sunny day. Can you see your shadow? Describe it.

- Does it have a colour?
- Can you see details of your face in your shadow?
- Is your shadow separated from your body? Or is it attached somewhere?

b How many shapes can you make with your shadow? Your shadow is where light does not go.

2

Play a tag game.

a Run around the playground. Try to jump on the head of another learner's shadow.

b Once someone has jumped on a shadow's head, the owner of that shadow is out of the game.

c Can you jump on the head of your own shadow? Why not?

Talk partners

a Talk to a partner about which shadow shapes you like best.

b Take a photograph or draw your favourite. Make a classroom display.

c Share your thoughts with the class.

hand shadow of an eagle

Transparent or opaque?

Think like a scientist!

You know that light travels in straight lines. Light shines through gaps in blinds.

Some materials block light. When light is blocked from a source, you can see a shadow.

light shining through gaps in blinds

Some objects are **transparent**. They let light through. You can see through transparent materials such as glass, water or air. They do not make good shadows.

Some objects are **opaque**. They do not let light pass through. We cannot see through them. Some objects that are made from opaque materials are wood, brick and metal. They make dark shadows. You are opaque. You make a good shadow!

1

Work with a partner.

a Tell each other what 'transparent' and 'opaque' mean.

b Decide which of these objects are transparent. Which are opaque? **Sort** them into two groups.

c Which objects have parts that are transparent and parts that are opaque?

Scientific words
transparent
opaque   sort

CD case

tennis ball

glass bottle

window

plastic cup

child

Investigating shadows

You will need...

- selection of materials of similar sizes (card, clear plastic, foil, fabric, tissue paper, cellophane, glass, leather, bubble wrap, ceramic, wood, metal) • ruler
- scissors • camera (optional) • torch

Be careful ⚠️

Take care when using glass.

a Work in a group. Collect the materials you will use. Use a ruler to measure carefully. Then cut the materials to the same size.

b Sort your materials into groups. Predict which materials will make a shadow. Which will not make a shadow?

c Make a list of your groups or take a photograph of them.

d Decide how you will test your materials.

e Test each material. You could put it in front of a light source such as a torch. How far away from the torch will you place your materials? Measure the distance carefully each time.

What will you need to keep the same to make the test fair?

f Make a table to **record** your **results**. Write down what you found out.

Material	Made shadow	Did not make shadow
foil	*yes, dark with good edges*	
clear plastic		*no, but some grey around edges*

g Talk to another group. Are your results the same?

h Go back to your prediction. Look at your groups. Should any materials be in a different group?

Scientific words

record   results

Fun with shadows

Think like a scientist!

Long ago, a man named Etienne de Silhouette, made portraits (pictures of faces) of people. He cut out the shape of their face from the side using black paper. The pictures looked like shadows. We call them silhouettes.

1

a Here are some silhouettes of animals. Try to name them.

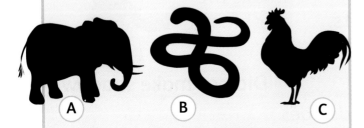

A   B   C

b Make your own animal silhouette. Draw the shape of an animal on black paper. Then cut it out and stick it onto a white background.

c Challenge a partner to name the animal.

2

You will need...
- lamp or torch

Make shadows indoors.

a Look at the picture. Use your hands to make an animal shape. Or make your own shape.

b Talk to a partner. What is blocking the light? Can your partner guess what animal shape you made?

3

You will need...
- aluminium foil   • torch

Make a model and silhouette.

- Model a shape from scrunched-up aluminium foil.

- Shine a light on your model to make a shadow.

- Draw around your model's shadow and colour it black.

- Now your model has its own silhouette!

What have you learnt about light and dark?

1

Mrs Ramirez has a bright, sunny classroom. Learners sometimes find it difficult to see because the light hurts their eyes.

a What can Mrs Ramirez do to make the classroom less sunny?

b Work with a partner. Write to Mrs Ramirez to tell her what she can do.

c Draw a picture of your ideas. Add labels.

What can you remember?

You have been learning about light and dark. Can you:

✔ name some sources of light?

✔ name some reflectors of light?

✔ describe what darkness is?

✔ describe how light travels?

✔ describe how shadows are made?

✔ recognise objects from the shape of the shadows they make?

✔ name some materials that make good shadows?

✔ sort opaque and transparent materials into groups?

Unit 5 Electricity

 ## What do you know about electricity?

Think like a scientist!

We use **electricity** all the time.
We use electricity to make things move.
We use it to make lamps light. We use
electricity to **heat** things. We also use it
make sounds or listen to music.
Electricity is very useful!

1

a Which of these six objects use
electricity? Write the names.

b Look around your school.
Draw the objects that use
electricity.

2

a Keep an 'electricity diary'
for a day. Write the names
of the electrical appliances
(machines that use electricity)
you use during the day.
Record when you use them.

b When do you use the most
electrical appliances? Is it in
the morning, afternoon or
evening?

c When do you use the fewest
electrical appliances?

Scientific words
electricity
heat

Is there a pattern in the way
your class uses electricity?
How can you find out?

Mains electricity

Think like a scientist!

Some appliances at home or school use **mains electricity**. This means they need to be plugged (fitted) into a **socket** to work.

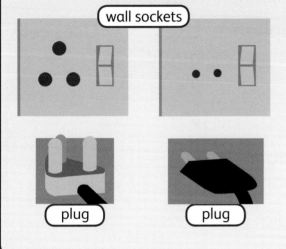

wall sockets

plug

plug

Large machines, such as these electrical appliances, often use mains electricity.

microwave oven

TV and remote

fridge

washing machine

We plug them into the electricity supply (where we get mains electricity) at a wall socket.

1

a Draw an outline of a home.

b Label the rooms.

c Draw some appliances that use mains electricity. Or, you could find pictures in old magazines and cut them out.

d Stick your pictures into the correct rooms in the home you drew.

e Which room has the most mains electricity appliances?

You will need...
- large sheet of paper/A3 sheet of paper
- old magazines
- scissors
- glue

Be careful ⚠

Never stick anything other than a plug into an electrical socket. The electricity could hurt you.

Scientific words

mains electricity
socket

Cell electricity

Scientific word
cells

Think like a scientist!

Some things in our homes use cells to make them work. **Cells** come in all shapes and sizes.

1

a Make a list of appliances.

b Record which appliances use mains electricity and which use cells. You could use a table like the one below.

Appliance	Uses mains electricity	Uses cells
lamp	✔	
mobile phone		✔
radio	✔	✔

c What other appliances can you think of that use either mains electricity or cells?

Be careful ⚠

Never cut open a cell. It can be very dangerous!

 What appliances could we use during a power cut? That is when there is no mains electricity.

Talk partners

Talk about the things you use that need cells to work.
a Make a list.
b Share your ideas with another pair.

Talk partners

Talk to a partner. What is similar about all the appliances that use cells?

Staying safe

Think like a scientist!

Electricity is very powerful. It helps us do many useful things. However, electricity can be very dangerous if we do not use it correctly.

Talk partners

Look carefully at this picture. Talk to a partner. How many dangers can you see? Write down your ideas.

1

Make a poster to show and explain some dangers of electricity.

Did you know?

Electricity travels at the speed of light – the fastest speed there is!

Using electricity

Think like a scientist!

You know that electricity can be mains or cell. You also know that we can use electricity to make things move, light up, heat up or make sounds. Electricity is very useful.

listening to music through headphones

1

Design an electrical machine or a **robot** – a human-like machine. Design it to help you do work around your home.

a Draw and label a picture of your robot.

b Include as many gadgets (tools) as you can.

c Write labels to show what your robot can do and how it works.

d Share your design with your group.

Talk partners

Imagine if there was no electricity in the world. Talk to a partner.
a What would you miss most? Why?
b Do you think you would like it if there was no electricity? Why?

Do some research to find out how electricity is used in transport. Think about trams, trains and electric cars.

Making electrical circuits

Think like a scientist!

A **circuit** is a path that electricity takes.
A circuit needs a **source** of electricity.
A source can be mains electricity or cells.
An electrical appliance needs a complete circuit to work.

Scientific words

circuit

source

components

different

1

Make a lamp light. The parts in a circuit are called **components**. They must be joined together.

*How many **different** ways can you find to light the lamp?*

Does it matter how you arrange the components?

What is the lowest number of components you could use?

You will need...
- lamp   • wires
- cell
- cell holder
- lamp holder
- crocodile clips

b Draw the circuit you have made to light the lamp.

c Label the components you used.

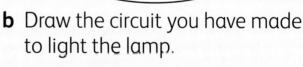

a Work in pairs. Use the equipment provided to light a lamp.

Talk partners

Talk to another pair. Explain what you have found out about circuits. Did you find out the same things?

Investigating components

Think like a scientist!

We make an electrical circuit by connecting components. This makes a path for electricity.

1

You will need...
• lamp • hand lens

a Look at a glass lamp with a hand lens. Draw what you see.

b Look for the wire running through the inside of the lamp.

c Look closely at the outside of the lamp. Find where the wire inside is attached to the outside of the lamp.

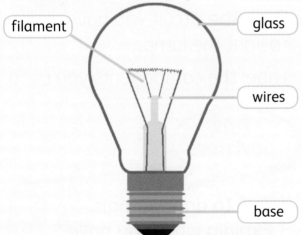

filament

glass

wires

base

Electricity moves *through* the lamp and makes the **filament** wires glow.

Be careful ⚠

Never squeeze a lamp. The glass is thin and could break.

2

a Look at the cell in the circuit you made on page 103. The ends of the cell are different. These are called **terminals**.

b Do you see the **symbol** (sign) at each terminal (+ and −)? The symbols help us to connect the correct terminal wires to the cell.

c What happens if you use just one terminal? Why do you think this happens? Use the scientific words.

Scientific words
filament
terminals
symbol

Exploring circuits

Think like a scientist!

To make a light work, electricity must flow (move easily) through the cells and through the lamp.

Scientific word
predict

1

You will need...
• circuit components

Stage 2 learners made some circuits. They drew diagrams of each circuit.

a In your group, **predict** which circuits will make the lamp light.

b Predict which circuits will not light the lamp. Why?

c Talk about what is needed to make circuits work.

d Make these circuits.

e Were your predictions correct?

f Think of a rule for making successful circuits.

2

Play this spinner game in pairs. Start with one cell. Take turns to spin and collect the component you land on.

a Who can make a complete circuit? How many components did you need to collect?

b Did anyone have a circuit with more than one lamp?

Making circuits work

Think like a scientist!

Sometimes a circuit has two cells in it. When this happens we must join the terminals in a certain order. The **positive (+)** terminal in the first cell must touch the **negative (–)** terminal in the second cell.

Talk partners

Is a component broken? What else could you check?

My circuit is not working but I am sure I have made it correctly.

Talk to a partner about why the circuit does not work. What should the learners check?

Scientific words

positive (+)
negative (–)

1

Write a checklist for learners to follow if their circuit does not work.

You will need...
• circuit components

2

Here are some drawings of circuits that do not work.

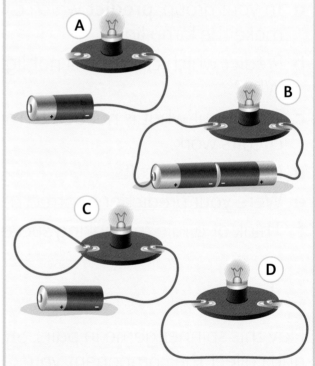

a Make these circuits yourself.

b What do you need to do to make them work?

c Write instructions for how to make each broken circuit work. Use scientific words.

Make a torch

Think like a scientist!

A torch often has more than one cell in it.

1

You will need...
- torch
- cells

Investigate torches.

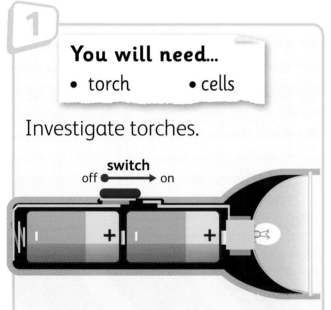

off ● switch → on

a An adult will help you to take a torch apart carefully.

b Look at each part. What is its job? Work out how each part makes the torch work.

c Draw a diagram to show how the torch works.

d Put your torch together again so that it works.

2

You will need...
- circuit components

a Use two cells to make a circuit. What happens to the lamp?

b Draw the circuit. What do you notice about the lamp? Write a sentence.

3

You will need...
- circuit components
- materials for the torch casing

Use your knowledge about circuits to make a torch.

a Gather the circuit components you will need to make your torch.

b How will you make your circuit?

c What will you use for the torch casing (the outside)?

d How successful was your torch?

e If you made another torch, what would you change to improve it?

Investigating batteries

Think like a scientist!

The scientific word for two or more cells in a circuit is a **battery**. We must put cells (batteries) into electrical appliances in a certain way to make them work.

Scientific word

battery

You will need...
- torch
- cells

2

a Look closely at the torch and cells (batteries) you used in Activity 1 on page 107.

b Draw and label the cells (batteries). Include the positive and negative terminals. Do you remember what these are?

c What will happen if the cells (batteries) are the wrong way around in a torch?

d Which terminals need to touch so that the electricity flows?

1

a Look carefully at this selection of cells (batteries).

b Match the cells (batteries) to the appliances.

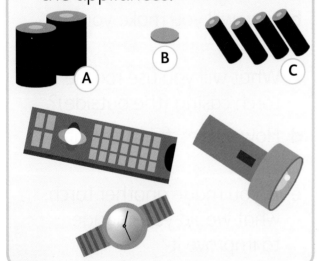

Talk partners

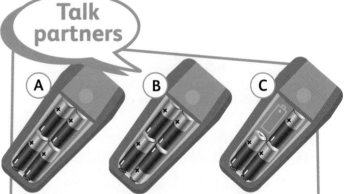

Look at these pictures of television remote controls.
a Talk to a partner about which ones will work.
b Which remote controls will not work. Why?
Share your ideas with another pair.

Broken circuits

Think like a scientist!

A break (gap) in a circuit means that electricity cannot move through the circuit.

You will need...
- balloon

Join another group for this game.

- Stand in a circle. This represents (is like) an electrical circuit.

- Pass the balloon to the person next to you in the circle. Do not use your hands!

- The balloon represents electricity moving through the electrical circuit.

- Your teacher will move two or three of you out of the circle to make a gap.

- This is a 'break' in the circuit. The electricity cannot get to the other side.

- When learners fill the gap, the balloon (electricity) can move along the circuit. The circle is complete once again.

You will need...
- drawing materials
- circuit components

Work with a partner.

a Draw a picture of a circuit with a lamp in it.

b Challenge your partner to explain if the circuit will light the lamp or not.

c Swap roles.

d Check your ideas by making the circuits. Were you right?

Useful broken circuits

Think like a scientist!

You know that if there is a break in a circuit it will not work.
Electricity needs an unbroken path to be able to flow.
If there is a break, the electricity cannot flow.
The circuit will not work.

1

You will need...
- lamp • lamp holder
- wires • cell • crocodile clips

a Make a circuit with a break in it, like this.

b Try it. The lamp will not light.

c Talk to your group. What must you do to make the lamp light?

d Explain (write reasons) why the open circuit (with a break in it) will not light the lamp.

Talk partners

Sometimes we need a circuit to have a break in it.
Talk to a partner about when a break in a circuit might be useful.
Here are some clues to help you.

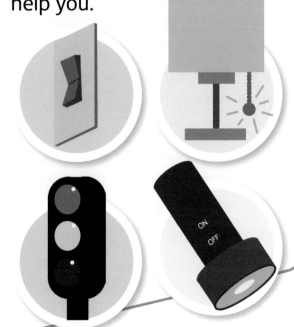

Switches

Think like a scientist!

We can use a **switch** to make or break a circuit.

When the switch is open, the circuit is broken.

When the switch is closed, the circuit is closed (complete). The electricity can flow.

2

Scientific word
switch

You will need...
- card
- paperclip
- split pins

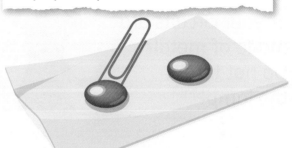

a Make a switch, as you can see in the picture.

b Put the switch in a simple circuit. Open and close the switch.

- For the switch to be closed, the metal paperclip must touch the metal pins.

- The electricity can now flow through the closed switch.

- The circuit is complete (closed).

c Draw your circuit with the switch open.

d Write some sentences to explain how the switch works.

1

a Look at this circuit.

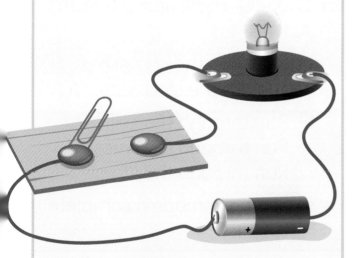

b Find the gap.

c Point to what can move to close the gap in this circuit. This is the switch.

d From what material is the switch made?

More about switches

Talk partners

Talk to a partner about the circuits you have made. Which parts of your circuits are made of metal? Do not forget the lamp!

Think like a scientist!

Switches are usually made of metal. Electricity flows easily through metal.

1

Go outside with your group.

Use chalk to draw a giant circuit on the playground. An adult will help you.

a Draw the cell and wires coming from it, to a lamp.

b Draw the wires that go inside the lamp to make it glow.

c Draw wires coming from the lamp, back to the cell.

2

a Use your chalk drawing from Activity 1.

• Stand on the chalk lines. You are the electricity.

• Run through the cell. Run through the wires. Run through the lamp.

• You have made a complete circuit.

b Make a break in the circuit. (Rub out some chalk.) Talk about what will happen to the electricity.

c Draw a switch and complete the circuit again. Talk about what will happen now.

Different switches

Talk partners

Talk to a partner.
a Make a list of all the electrical appliances you know that have switches.
b When is it important to turn off electrical appliances?

1

Anika wrote to her grandmother to tell her what she had done at school.

Dear Nana

Today I made a pressure switch in school.

I glued two pieces of foil on the inside of a folded piece of card.

Then I put wires under each piece of foil. The wires were part of my circuit.

When I pushed the foil together I made the circuit complete. My lamp lit up!

Here is a picture of what I did.

Lots of love

Anika

You will need...
- wires
- cell (battery)
- lamp
- lamp holder
- aluminium foil
- card

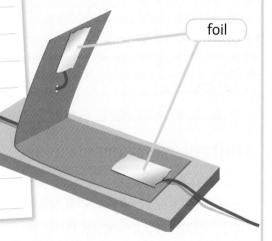

foil

a Follow Anika's instructions to make a pressure switch.

b Use your switch in a circuit with a lamp.

Making switches

Scientific word
buzzer

Talk partners

Rohan's sister Jaya is always sneaking into his room.
Rohan made an alarm so he can hear when Jaya goes into his bedroom.
Here is the switch he made.
It is called a pressure switch.
Talk to a partner. How does Rohan's alarm work?

1

Jaya made her own alarm. She made a trip-wire switch.

When Rohan's foot trips over the thread, the thread pulls on the foil ball.
The foil ball closes the circuit. The **buzzer** sounds.

Make a trip-wire switch.

Hint: Buzzers sometimes only work one way around in a circuit. If yours does not buzz, try connecting it the other way around.

You will need...
- thread
- wire
- closed card tube (such as a film case or sweets tube)
- aluminium foil
- paperclip wires
- cells (batteries)
- buzzer

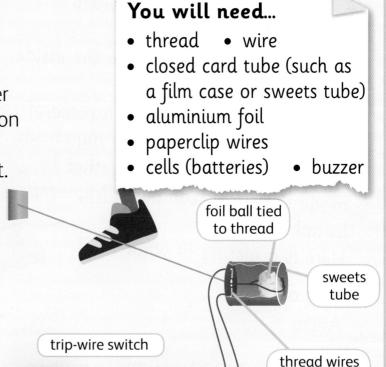

foil ball tied to thread

sweets tube

trip-wire switch

thread wires bent over to form contacts

Make a wobbly game

1

You are going to make a wobble detector (finder).

- Make lots of bends in the stiff wire.

- Fill the lids with modelling dough. Push one end of the stiff wire into each lid.

- Attach one end of the stiff wire to the copper wire. Attach the copper wire to the cells (battery).

- Connect (join) another wire to the cells (battery) and the buzzer.

- Bend the end of your last wire into a loop (circle).

- Put the loop around the end of the stiff wire.

- Move the loop along the bends without touching the stiff wire.

- When the wires touch, your circuit is complete. Electricity should flow and the buzzer will sound!

You will need...

- two lids from jars
- modelling dough
- bendable stiff bare wire (such as coat hanger wire)
- buzzer
- sticky tape
- cells (battery)
- three pieces of copper (a type of metal) wire

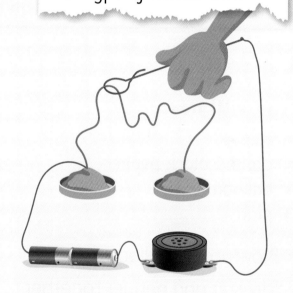

Can you get to the end without sounding the buzzer? Use a timer to see who will be quickest!

115

Static electricity

Scientific words
static electricity

Think like a scientist!

We can control electricity in circuits. We can add components and use switches to control how we use the electricity.

Another type of electricity is **static electricity**. This is difficult to control but it can be fun!

When we rub two materials together, we produce static electricity. This can cause static electricity to build up.

Static electricity can give you a shock when you touch a car door or travel on an escalator.

Static electricity is making this child's hair stand up!

1

You will need...
- salt
- ground black pepper
- balloon
- plate

- Blow up the balloon.
- Mix salt and pepper together on a plate.
- Rub the balloon 20 times on your hair or on a jumper.
- Hold the balloon about 2 cm above the salt and pepper mixture.

What happens?

Talk partners

a Talk to your group about what you think is happening in Activity 1.

b Have you ever had a shock from static electricity? Talk about it.

What have you learnt about electricity?

1

Work in pairs on this competition!

a Read the instructions and talk about your ideas.

Competition instructions

- Use what you know about circuits and switches to make a model.
- Design a model car with a simple circuit in it.
- You might want to add a switch. Then you can turn it on or off.
- Make your model and test it.

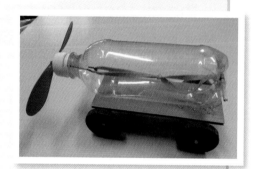

b The pictures show some models made by other learners. What will yours be like?

What can you remember?

You have been learning about electricity. Can you:

✔ name some uses of electricity?

✔ describe how electricity can be dangerous and how we can use it safely?

✔ name some components of a circuit?

✔ describe the path of electricity in a circuit?

✔ construct a simple circuit to light a lamp?

✔ describe what a switch does?

✔ explain why some simple circuits work and others do not?

Unit 6 The Earth and beyond

⟳ Beyond the Earth

Think like a scientist!

The Earth is our home **planet**.
Beyond the Earth is **space**.
Space begins where the Earth's **atmosphere** ends. The atmosphere is the air that surrounds the Earth.
Not even scientists know where space ends.

our planet Earth

Scientific words
planet
space
atmosphere

1

Have you ever looked up at the night sky? Did you wonder what is up there?

You will find out. You are going on a journey into space!

a Talk in your group. What do you think you will need to be able to go into space?

b How will you get there?

c What will you eat and drink?

d Will you need special clothes?

e Draw some pictures of how you will get to space. Show what you will wear and what you will need to take with you.

2

a Are you ready to go? Let's pretend.

b Sit in your rocket. Put on your helmet.

c Check your controls.

d Start the countdown: 10...9...8...7...6...5...4...3...2...1.... ...BLAST OFF!

This spaceship is blasting off to outer space!

What is space?

Think like a scientist!

Space is huge! Most of space is empty but there are planets and **stars**.

There are many stars in space!

1

Imagine that you are starting your journey.

a Look out of your rocket window.

b Can you see the stars? Can you see the **Sun**?

Scientific words

stars

Sun

universe

heat

2

The Sun is the closest star to the Earth.
It gives us light and **heat**. Most stars are bigger than our Sun. They look tiny because they are so far away.

the Sun

Learn this rhyme with a partner:

The Sun is in the sky

The Sun is in the sky

Hot and bright

It gives us light

The Sun is in the sky.

Did you know?

There are more stars in the **universe** than grains of sand on all the beaches on Earth!

3

a Write down other facts you know about the Sun.

b Share these with your group.

The solar system

Think like a scientist!

You will now learn more about the planets and the star closest to us.
The Sun is the closest star to our planet, Earth.
The Earth and other planets move around the Sun.
We call the Sun and planets around it the **solar system**.

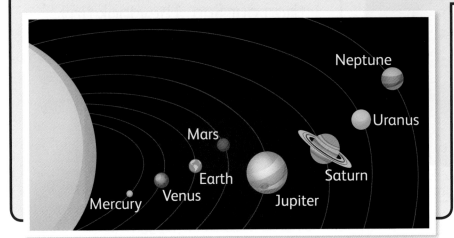

Neptune

Uranus

Mars

Earth

Saturn

Mercury   Venus   Jupiter

Do other planets have moons?

1

a Make a mini-book about the solar system.

b You could make it in the shape of a planet or rocket.

c Use collage materials to illustrate your front cover.

d Find out some facts about the Sun and the planets. Add the facts to your mini-book.

e Share your mini-book with your group.

2

a Use your research skills. Find out one amazing fact about each planet in our solar system.

b Talk about your facts with your group.

c Which is your favourite planet? Why?

Scientific words
solar system

⟳ Planets and their orbits

Think like a scientist!

The Sun is at the centre of the solar system.

Eight planets and a dwarf planet called Pluto travel around the Sun.

The circular (round) journey each planet makes is its orbit.

a planet's orbit around the Sun

1

The solar system is enormous. Pretend to be the planets!

You will need...
- big yellow balloon
- group of 10 learners

- Go outside.
- Person 1 must hold a big yellow balloon to represent the Sun.
- Person 2 stands right next to the Sun to represent the first planet, Mercury. It is closest to the Sun.
- Venus is next and must stand one arm's length from the Sun.
- Continue adding 'planets'. Will you have enough space?

- Ask your teacher to take a photograph of your human solar system.

Scientific word
compare

2

Can you remember the name of the path of a planet around the Sun? The answer is an orbit.

a Make your human planets orbit the Sun.

b Look at the orbits of the planets closest to the Sun. **Compare** these with the planets furthest away. What do you notice?

The Earth spins

Scientific words
axis
North Pole
South Pole

Think like a scientist!

The Earth spins. It goes around on its **axis**.
The Earth's axis is an imaginary line. It goes
from the **North Pole** at the top to the **South Pole** at the bottom.

1

You will need...
• globe

Look at a globe. A globe is
a model of the Earth.

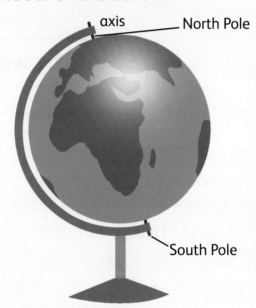

axis — North Pole

South Pole

a Point to the Poles.

b Imagine a line that goes
from the North Pole at the
top. It continues through the
centre of the Earth to the
South Pole at the bottom.

c Draw a picture of the globe
model of the Earth.

d Look carefully. Notice that the
line is tilted to one side. This is
called the Earth's axis.

e Add labels to your drawing.
Use the scientific words in
the box.

Talk partners

Talk to a partner.
a Do you feel as if you are
spinning around? Even
though the Earth spins
we do not feel it.
b Think of other
things you know
that spin. Make
a list.

The way the Earth spins

Think like a scientist!

The Earth spins in one direction.
We say that the Earth spins anticlockwise.

You are still travelling in space.

On your space journey you can see the Earth.

Look down at the North Pole. You can see that the Earth spins in only one direction. That is anticlockwise.

a Look at a clock face. Notice the direction that the hands move. We call this direction 'clockwise'. It means 'like a clock'.

The Earth spins in the opposite direction to the hands of a clock. This is anticlockwise. 'Anti' means against.

b Pretend that you are the spinning Earth. Stretch your arms out to your sides. Now carefully spin anticlockwise. Take care not to get too dizzy! The Earth spins like this:

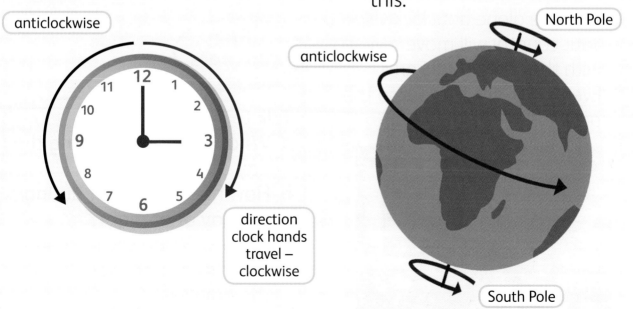

anticlockwise

direction clock hands travel – clockwise

anticlockwise

North Pole

South Pole

A day on the Earth

Scientific word
rotation

Think like a scientist!

The Earth takes one day (24 hours) to make a complete **rotation** (spin) on its axis.

One rotation means that it takes 24 hours (one day) for a place on Earth to return to the position where it started.

 1

You will need...
• globe

Use a globe to show one rotation of the Earth.

a Find your home country.

b Spin the globe anticlockwise. Your country will move with the spin of the Earth. Eventually, it will return to the position where it started.

 2

You will need...
• strip of paper
• glue or sticky tack or putty

Make a 'day and night' wrist band.

a Fold a strip of paper in two.

b On one side of the fold line, draw things you do in the day. On the other side, draw things you do at night.

c Join the strip together to make a band.

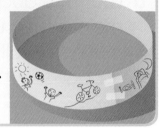

Talk partners

Talk to a partner.
a What can you do during the day and at night?
b How hot or cold is it during the day or at night?
c What can you see at night that you cannot see during the day?

Day and night

Scientific word
different

Think like a scientist!

The Earth takes one day, or 24 hours, to spin once.
The spinning of the Earth gives us day and night.
The Sun does not move.
When part of the Earth faces the Sun, it is light. It is daytime.
When part of the Earth faces away from the Sun, it is dark. It is night time.

1

Model how the Earth spins.
Work in a group.

a Stick the plastic figure onto your country on the globe. In a dark place, shine the torch onto the globe. The torch is the light from the Sun.

You will need...
- globe or ball (or orange on a stick that can spin)
- strong torch
- small plastic figure
- sticky tack or putty

b Notice where the light falls onto the globe. Is the whole globe lit?

c Keep the torch (the Sun) still. Spin the Earth gently on its axis.

d Notice which part of the globe is lit by the light now. Is the figure in light (day) or dark (night)?

e Spin the globe gently again. Which part of the Earth is lit now?

f Make a complete rotation of the Earth. Notice how **different** countries are in the light at different times.

More about day and night

Think like a scientist!

You know that the Sun is our main **source** of light (where light comes from).

As the Earth spins, parts of it move in and out of the Sun's light. This gives us day and night.

the Sun shining in a desert

1

Look at a globe and find where you live.

a Imagine a line through the Earth – from where you live to the other side.

b Where is opposite you on the globe?

Scientific word
source

2

Your class is going to model how we get day and night.

- Go outside to a large space. Stand in a large circle and join hands.

- Turn to face outwards from the circle.

- Your teacher will be the Sun. Your teacher will stand outside the circle. To show where the Sun's light is shining, your teacher will hold a torch.

- In the circle, move slowly to your left. Move anticlockwise.

- Keep moving anticlockwise until you are back where you started.

- This is like the Earth turning during a day. When you can see the Sun it is daytime. When you cannot see the Sun it is night time.

Tracking the Sun

Think like a scientist!

The Sun appears in different places in the sky at different times of the day.

Scientific word
predict

1

You will need...
- yellow and orange tissue paper
- sticky tape
- clock

Do this investigation over two days.

a Talk about where you see the Sun in the sky at different times of the day.

b Does it always look as if it is in the same place?

c Find a sunny classroom with a window. **Predict** where you will see the Sun at different times of the day.

d Stick a circle of yellow tissue paper on the window. Place it where you think the Sun will be in the morning, at midday and in the afternoon. If you

wish, add more times during the day. Take a photograph of, or draw, your prediction.

e Look at this prediction that some Stage 2 learners made:

f Now put an orange circle of paper where the Sun actually is at different times. Do this every two hours.

g Were you right? Take a photograph of, or draw, your results. Compare your results with your prediction.

Can you believe your eyes?

Think like a scientist!

The Sun appears to move across the sky. The Sun does not move but the Earth does!

My teacher says the Sun does not move. How can it be in different places at different times of the day?

The Sun stays in the same place. We are moving. The Earth is spinning.

1

Work with a partner.

a Stand about two metres apart. Face each other. One person is the Sun and must not move. The other person is the Earth.

b The Earth should make a one-quarter turn anticlockwise. Now the Earth has the Sun on its right side.

c The Earth makes another one-quarter turn. Now the Earth has the Sun behind it.

d The Earth makes another one-quarter turn. Now the Sun is to the left of the Earth.

e The Earth makes a final one-quarter turn. The Earth and the Sun are back at the beginning. The Sun has not moved. It just seemed to be in different places from where the Earth was.

Talk partners

Talk to a partner.
a Have you ever travelled by car or train? When you looked out of the window did the land appear to move? We know it did not. You were moving! That is like the Sun and the Earth.
b Why does it look as if the Sun moves, when we know it does not?

Investigating with shadow sticks

Think like a scientist!

The Sun is a source of light.
Shadows form when light is blocked.
Shadows can be different at different times of the day.

1

Work with a partner. You will investigate how shadows can change.

You will need...
• pencil
• sticky tack or putty
• torch

a Stick down your pencil with sticky tack or putty.

b Use your torch to make a shadow of the pencil.

c Make the shortest and longest shadows you can. Where is the light source?

d Make your pencil shadow on the right-hand side. Where is the light source?

e Where must the light source be to make a shadow on the left-hand side?

f Compare two shadows. Draw pictures.

g Write a sentence about what you have observed.

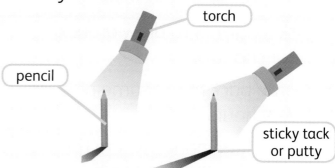

torch

pencil

sticky tack or putty

Talk partners

Talk to a partner.
a Imagine that the Sun is directly overhead. Use your observations to predict what shadows will look like.
b Imagine that the Sun is very low in the sky (close to the land). What will shadows look like then?

Recording shadow changes

1

During the day, sunlight comes from different directions. Work with a partner.

- Stand in a sunny part of the playground in the early morning.

- Remember where you are standing and where the Sun is. Chalk a mark on the ground.

- Ask a partner to draw around your shadow.

- Come back to the same place every hour.

- Every hour, notice where the Sun is. Ask your partner to draw around your shadow.

Here is Dev's shadow drawing. Does yours look like this?

Talk partners

Talk to a partner.
Compare your shadows.

a What do you notice about the length and direction of your shadows as the day goes on?

b When is your shadow the shortest? Where is the Sun at this time?

c When is your shadow the longest? Where is the Sun at this time?

2

Dev recorded his shadow changing, like this.

Do something similar.

The Moon

Think like a scientist!

So far, the Moon is the only place in space that people have visited.

People who explore space are called astronauts.

the Moon

Talk partners

Talk to a partner. Imagine that you are going to the Moon.
a What will you need?
b Which of these things will you take with you. Why?

1

Astronauts have visited the Moon. We cannot live on the Moon yet.

a Why do you think this is? Write down your ideas.

b Share your ideas with your group. Do you have the same ideas?

astronauts on the Moon

Talk partners

Talk to a partner.
a Can you see any shapes in the Moon? Some people can see a face. Others can see a rabbit. What can you see?
b Share your ideas with another pair.

Walking on the Moon

Think like a scientist!

The Moon is Earth's **satellite**. A satellite is something that **orbits** (goes around) a planet. The Moon orbits the Earth.

What do you think it is like on the Moon?

1

In space, the Moon is the closest object to Earth. Only 12 people have walked on the Moon!

a Use your research skills to find out about missions (trips) to the Moon.

b Who was the first person to walk on the Moon?

c Make a poster about the Moon.

Scientific words

satellite
orbits

2

You will need...
• 'space stilts'

Walking on the Moon is difficult. There is no air to breathe. You have to wear a special space suit. The space suit makes it hard to move around.

a Try using special space stilts. Imagine that you can feel what walking on the Moon might be like. Compare the feeling to walking on Earth.

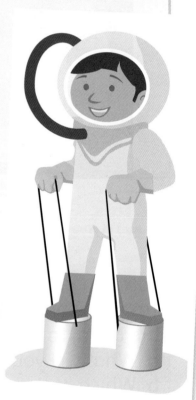

b How quickly can you move? Time yourself walking normally. Then time yourself walking with stilts. Which is faster?

Moon craters

Think like a scientist!

Scientific words
craters
asteroids

People used to think the Moon had a smooth surface. A scientist named Galileo looked at the Moon through a telescope 400 years ago.

He saw rocks, dust and **craters**! Craters are bowl-shaped hollows. They are made after **asteroids** have crashed into the surface. Asteroids are huge lumps of rock travelling through space.

1

Work in a group to investigate craters.

a Smooth the sand in your tray so you have a flat surface. Sprinkle it with powder paint (to help you see the craters).

b Put the tray on the floor. Stand up and drop a marble into the tray. What do you notice?

c Drop the marble from different heights. Drop a ball instead of a marble. What happens? Compare different sizes or weights of balls.

d Share what you have found out with other groups.

You will need...
- tray of sand or flour
- powder paint
- marbles, selection of balls
- ruler
- tape measure

a crater

Stars, galaxies and constellations

Think like a scientist!

There are billions of stars in the universe. Stars are enormous balls of burning **gas**. They give off heat and light. Millions of stars together make a **galaxy**.

A pattern of stars in a galaxy is a **constellation**.

We are here.

1

Ancient **astronomers** (scientists who study space) gave names to patterns of stars they saw in the sky. They thought some looked like animals.

Look at the picture of the constellation called Leo (lion). Astronomers imagined lines between the stars. They made the shape of a lion – like a 'join the dots' game.

Make your own constellation.

You will need...
- black paper
- white paint
- tracing paper

a Make some dots on black paper with white paint. These are your stars. Let them dry.

b Put some tracing paper over your constellation. Join your star dots with lines to make a shape.

c What does your shape look like? Give your constellation a name.

What is our galaxy called?

Scientific words
gas
galaxy
constellation
astronomers

More about the solar system

Think like a scientist!

You are still on your journey through space. Now you need a plan of the solar system to show you how to get home!

1

Make a model of the solar system.

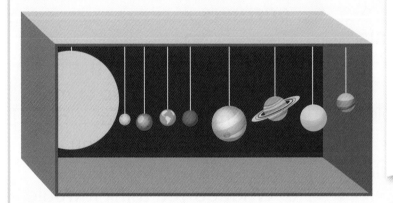

You will need...
- shoebox or other card box
- card
- scissors
- black paint
- coloured paints
- string
- sticky tape

- Draw the Sun and planets on card.
- Colour and cut them out.
- Paint the inside of your box black.
- Attach thread to each planet. Hang them in the correct order in your box.

Remember: Some planets are bigger than others.

Talk partners Talk to a partner.
a Which planets will you pass on your journey back to Earth from the Sun?
b Many planets are named after gods and goddesses. Find out who Neptune and Mars were.
c If you could name a planet, what would you call it? Why?

Exploring space

Think like a scientist!

Scientists have sent **rockets** and space probes to other planets in our solar system. Look at the space probe (machine) in the picture.

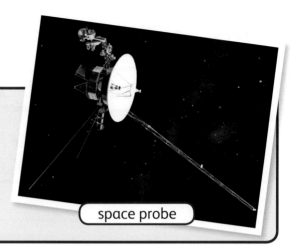

space probe

1

You see two job advertisements. One is for an astronaut to go into space. The other is for a scientist to stay on Earth to plan the mission (trip).

a Choose which job you would like to apply for.

Wanted – astronaut

Wanted – mission planner

b Write a letter. Explain why you would be the right person for the job.

Hint: What sort of person goes into space? Is it a brave, fit person? What sort of person would make a good mission planner? Are they careful and thoughtful?

Talk partners

Some people believe there is alien life on other planets. 'Alien' means life that is not from Earth. What do you think? Talk to a partner.

a What do you think it would it be like if aliens visited Earth?

b Would it be a good thing or not?

2

Design a travel brochure for an alien about our solar system.

What have you learnt about the Earth and beyond?

1

Mariam wrote her address like this:

Mariam Dossary

Hamza Villas 123

Road 55

Isa Town

Bahrain

Asia

Planet Earth

Solar system

Milky Way galaxy

Universe

Write your address in the same way.

What can you remember?

You have been learning about the Earth and beyond. Can you:
- ✔ name and order the planets in the solar system?
- ✔ describe what an orbit is and give an example?
- ✔ describe one way that the Earth moves in space?
- ✔ describe how we get day and night?
- ✔ describe how the Sun appears to move during the day?
- ✔ describe how shadows can change during the day?

1 Copy and complete the sentence. Choose the correct word.

loss   absence   brightness   reflection

Where there is no light, it is dark. We say that darkness is the _____ of light.

2 The lamp in this circuit will not light. Explain why.

3 How long does it take the Earth to spin once on its axis?

4 Which of these circuits will work?

a

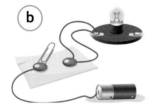
b

c

5 Which of these are sources of light?

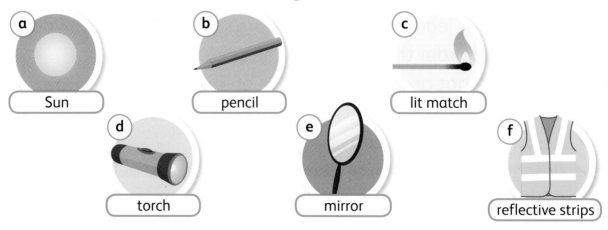

a — Sun

b — pencil

c — lit match

d — torch

e — mirror

f — reflective strips

6 Write the names of two appliances that use mains electricity.

7   Ali wants to make a shadow with some materials he found.
     Which materials would make good shadows?

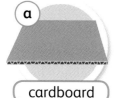
cardboard

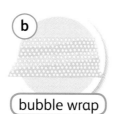
bubble wrap

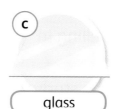
glass

wood

8   Diego made a circuit.
     The circuit did not work.
     The lamp did not light.
     What must Diego do to
     make the circuit work?

9   Write two things that use cell (battery) electricity.

10   Look at the drawing of our solar system. Write labels for **a**, **b** and **c**.

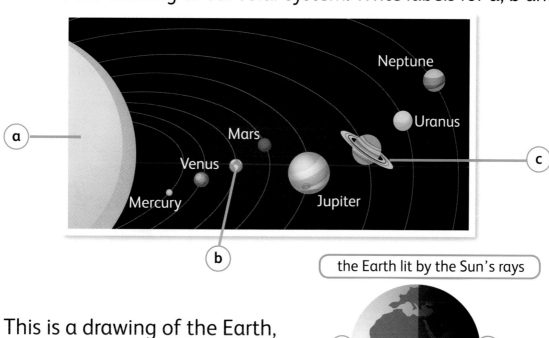

the Earth lit by the Sun's rays

11   This is a drawing of the Earth,
     as seen from space.
     a Where is it day – at A, B or C?
     b Where is it night – at A, B or C?

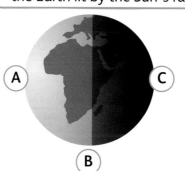

Scientific dictionary

A

Absence Lack of something

Asteroids Large rocks travelling in orbit around the Sun

Astronomers Scientists who study space

Atmosphere The gas that surrounds planet Earth

Axis The imaginary line that the Earth is spinning around

B

Battery Two or more cells placed end to end in a circuit

Bioluminescence Where living things such as glow-worms and some sea creatures produce their own light

Blizzard This happens when there is a lot of snow and wind

Brightness/bright Not dim, full of light

Buzzer An electrical component that makes a noise when electricity flows through it

C

Cells Sources of electricity for smaller electrical appliances

Circuit A cell, battery, wires or other electrical components all joined in a loop (circle) that electricity can flow around

Classify To sort into groups and name

Cocoons Casings of silk thread spun to protect a developing insect

Coir Natural fibres from coconut shells, used for floor mats and brushes

Compare To note similarities and differences between two things

Components Anything in an electrical circuit

Constellation A particular group of stars

Cools When a substance gets colder

Craters Large holes on a planet or moon made by a meteorite crashing into the surface

Crystals Tiny, transparent, coloured or glass-like shapes, sometimes found in rocks

crystals

D

Dark Little or no light

Different Not the same as

Dim Not bright, a lack of light

Dissolve When a solid seems to disappear in a liquid

E

Electricity A flow through wires that makes electric appliances work

Endangered At risk, threatened with extinction

Environment The local area, weather and landscape in which something lives

Erupts When molten (melted) rock pushes through the Earth's surface out of a volcano

Extinct An animal or plant that no longer exists, that has died out

F

Fabric A type of cloth made by weaving such as cotton, wool or linen

Filament In electrical components, a thin wire in a lamp that glows when electricity flows through it

Fossils The remains of ancient living things left as marks in rocks

Freeze To become ice, cooling something until it becomes solid

G

Galaxy A large group of stars, close together in space – our galaxy is the Milky Way

Gas A state of matter, gas is a substance that can spread all around and is usually invisible (such as oxygen and helium)

Geologist A scientist who studies rocks

Groups Collections of things that are similar in some way

H

Habitat Where a plant or animal lives

Heat Increase the temperature of something, make hotter

Hibernation/hibernate To slow down or sleep through the winter months

Hurricane A big storm with strong winds and lots of rain – can cause a lot of damage

hurricane

I

Identify To give a name to something, to recognise

Invertebrates Animals without a backbone

Irreversible Cannot change back to the way it was

L

Lava Liquid rock flowing down the sides of a volcano that has erupted

Light Something (such as sunlight) or a lamp that lets us see objects

141

Light rays Lines used to show the direction in which light travels

Liquid A state of matter, a liquid is a runny substance that does not have a fixed shape (such as water)

F

Mains electricity Electricity supplied to houses and schools from a power station

Man-made Not natural

Materials Everything is made of materials such as wood, paper, metal

Melt To heat a solid material so that it becomes runny

Meteorologists Scientists who study the weather

Micro-habitat Part of a habitat that is very small, for example, under a stone in a desert habitat

Migration/migrate When animals move from one part of the world

Molten Very hot, liquid rock

Monsoon A season in certain parts of the world, when there is very heavy rain, thunderstorms and floods

Moon – the Earth's satellite orbiting the planet every 28 days

Moon

N

Natural Found in nature, not artificial or man-made

Negative (–) Opposite of positive, the terminal on a cell from which electricity flows

Nocturnal Active at night, asleep or resting during the day

North Pole The point in the North where the Earth's axis meets the surface (at the top)

O

Observe To look carefully using all the senses to learn something

Opaque Materials that will not let light pass through

Orbit The path the Earth or other planets follow around the Sun, or the Moon around the Earth

Ores Any types of rocks that contain metal, for example, iron ore, copper ore

P

Patterns A repeated design or set of numbers where you can predict what comes next

Pebbles Small, generally smooth rocks

Planet A large object that orbits the Sun, for example, Neptune, Mars, Earth

Plastic A man-made material

Pollution When harmful objects or substances are introduced into the environment

Positive (+) Opposite of negative, a terminal on a cell

Prediction/Predict What you think will happen, based on what you already know about something

Process To change a material so that it can be used, or, a way of doing, or making, something that follows a particular order

Properties The way a material behaves, for example, one property of a solid material is that it keeps its shape

R

Rain gauge Used top measure how much rain has fallen

Record To write down or take a photograph

rain gauge

Recycle To use again or change in some way to make something new

Reflect When light bounces off a surface

Reflection What we see in a mirror or in a smooth or shiny surface

Results The outcomes of our investigations

Reversible A change that can be changed back

Robot A machine that can do jobs or work and is controlled by a computer

Rotation To turn around a point or around an axis (vertical line)

Rubber A natural elastic and waterproof liquid from a tropical tree – rubber can be made into car tyres and wellington boots

S

Satellite Anything that orbits a planet, for example, the Moon

Scale A regular series of steps or measures

Scale of hardness A scale to measure how hard different rocks are – invented by Friedrich Mohs, a German geologist

Senses Sight, hearing, touch, taste and smell – how we find out about the world around us

Shadows Dark shapes on a surface, made by opaque objects blocking light

Shiny Sparkly, glittery material that reflects light well

Similar Alike but not identical, looking or being almost the same

Smelting Remove metal from its ore by heating and melting

Socket A device in a wall where a plug from an appliance is inserted (pushed) to connect to a supply of electricity

Soil A mixture of tiny ground-down pieces of rock, dead plants, water and air

Solar system The Sun and the planets and their moons that orbit the Sun

Solidify To change state from a liquid into a solid, usually by cooling

Solid A state of matter, a solid keeps its shape and volume and does not flow

Sort Put into groups, classify

Source The start or beginning, where something comes from, for example, the Sun is a source of light

South Pole The point in the South where the Earth's axis meets the surface (at the bottom)

South Pole

Space Anything beyond Earth's atmosphere

Species Living things that look alike and can reproduce (have babies)

Stars Huge balls of burning gases in space, seen as lights in the night sky

Static electricity Electricity that does not flow through a circuit, it can build up on an object and gives us an electric shock

Stone A piece of rock

Sun Earth's nearest star and most important source of light

Switch A component which can make a gap in an electrical circuit to turn other components on or off

Symbol A sign or drawing that stands for something

T

Temperature How hot or cold something is, measured using a thermometer in degrees Celsius (°C)

Terminals The ends of an electrical cell where wires are attached in a circuit

Textures How something feels to the touch, for example, rough, smooth

Thermometer An instrument used to measure temperature

Transparent A material that is able to let light pass through it

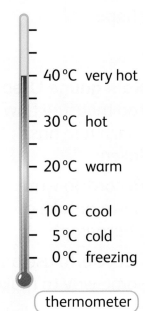

40°C very hot

30°C hot

20°C warm

10°C cool

5°C cold

0°C freezing

thermometer

U

Universe Everything in space

V

Volcano A mountain with a hole at the top where hot, liquid rock is forced out from under the ground

W

Wood A natural material from the trunk and branches of trees